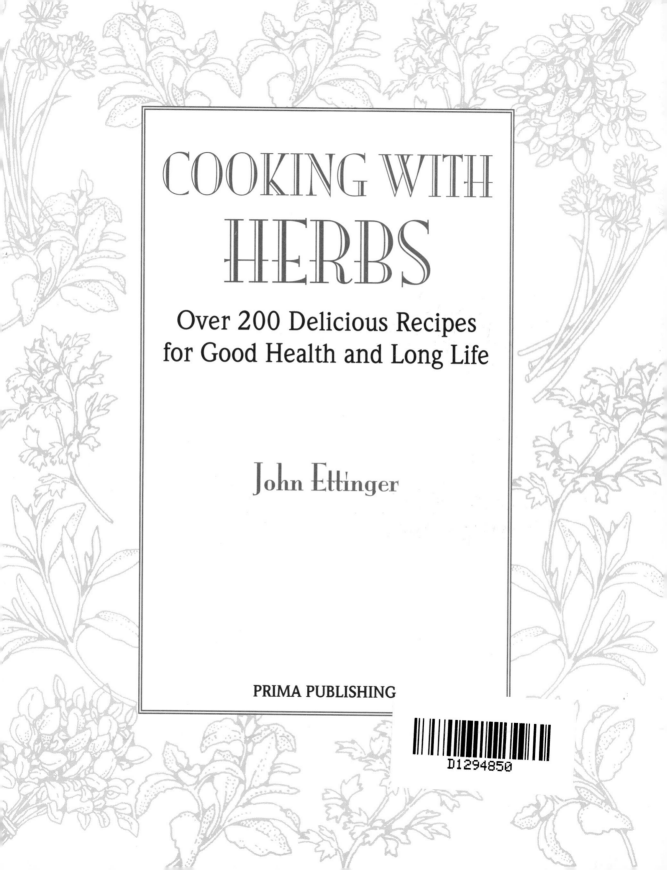

COOKING WITH
HERBS

Over 200 Delicious Recipes
for Good Health and Long Life

John Ettinger

PRIMA PUBLISHING

PRIMA PUBLISHING and colophon are trademarks of Prima Communications, Inc.

Library of Congress Cataloging-in-Publication Data

Ettinger, John.
    Cooking with herbs : over 200 delicious recipes for good health and long
      life / John Ettinger.
      p.   cm.
      Includes index.
      ISBN 0-7615-0244-0
      1. Cookery (Herbs)   2. Herbs.   I. Title.
TX819.H4E88   1996
641.6'57--dc20   96-225
                                                        CIP

96 97 98 99 00 AA 10 9 8 7 6 5 4 3 2 1
Printed in the United States of America

About the Nutritional Information
A per serving nutritional breakdown is provided for each recipe. If a range is given for an ingredient amount, the breakdown is based on the smaller number. If a range is given for servings, the breakdown is based on the larger number. If a choice of ingredients is given in an ingredient listing, the breakdown is calculated using the first choice. Nutritional content may vary depending on the specific brands or types of ingredients used. "Optional" ingredients, or those for which no specific amount is stated, are not included in the breakdown. Nutritional figures are rounded to the nearest whole number.

How to Order:
Single copies may be ordered from Prima Publishing, P.O. Box 1260BK, Rocklin, CA 95677; telephone (916) 632-4400. Quantity discounts are also available. On your letterhead, include information concerning the intended use of the books and the number of books you wish to purchase.

Contents

Contents

CINNAMON   69

CORIANDER/CILANTRO   83

CUMIN   105

DILL   115

Contents

MUSTARD   187

OREGANO   191

PARSLEY   201

Contents

Acknowledgments

I was able to write this book thanks to wonderful contributions from friends Judy Jacobsen, Penny Kozar, Brenda Lawrence, John Lien, Velma Tepper, and Valerie Wicklund. I'm grateful for the careful copyediting (once again) of Marianne Rogoff, the patience and support of my editor, Alice Anderson, and continuing encouragement from Amy Driscoll, my sons, Andrew and Joseph, and my sister, Virginia Phillips.

Introduction

Cookbooks of the 1950s suggested an electric mixer was essential equipment. In the 1970s, besides the ubiquitous fondue pot, a microwave became the must-have accessory. Both of these appliances spoke to the desire to reduce cooking time. Obviously, we were more interested in making cooking less of a chore, whether the quality of the food suffered or not.

Times and tastes march forward, which is fortunate for those of us who never understood the fascination with fondue. Today's fresh cooking requires utensils that save time and get the most from fresh ingredients. Here are three I don't think any kitchen should be without:

- **Citrus zester** This handy device lets you quickly zest those lemons, limes, and oranges. Zest adds the flavor that is only hinted at by the juice of the fruit.
- **Ginger grater** Here is another inexpensive item that makes cooking so much easier. Ginger is difficult to grate without a special grater, and clean-up with this device is just a quick rinse.
- **A good garlic press** That is, one that allows you to mince without peeling the garlic. This is the most costly of the three, but it's more than worth it. Not having to peel those cloves saves a lot of time and hassle.

For the style of cooking I do, these three are truly essential. I use a considerable amount of zest, ginger, and garlic in my dishes and without these helpful gadgets I'd still be in the kitchen cooking, rather than writing.

That these three items are important for today's cooking also reflects the increasing desire to eat healthful, good-tasting foods—time constraints notwithstanding. Increasingly, we are returning to the ways of our grandparents as we recognize how a meal can be a gathering and the joy is not only in the taking of the food, but in the preparation as well. We have all observed at one time or another that no matter how large the house, everyone seems to gather in the kitchen.

I came to cooking relatively late, a little more than a decade ago, but I approached it with time to learn and a great deal of enthusiasm. My interest in the health effects of food goes back at least fifteen years when my first son was affected by the artificial ingredients placed in many foods. At the age of two, Andrew's temperament became stormy and his color faded if he ate junk. I began reading labels and avoiding many foods that carried the ingredients affecting Andrew. It was startling to learn how many false ingredients there were in foods, and how little long-term research had been done on their effects, especially when it came to children. Most safe amounts had been calculated for adults.

My second son, Joseph, came along eight years later and he was allergic to milk, corn, and soy. Not a good combination since corn syrup, dairy of one sort or another, and soy byproducts are ingredients in almost every packaged food. It was then I wrote a cookbook about using sauces without butter or cream—sauces I could feed to Joseph.

Beyond that I learned about the healing power of herbs for my son's upset stomach. Ginger, a healer for centuries in China, Japan, and India, worked well to ease his stomach distress. I continue to serve it, although at nine he has outgrown most of his allergies.

The use of healing foods is ongoing in our home. Whenever one or the other has a cold they can expect to find plenty of garlicky foods on their plates—to cure one and prevent the other from catching the cold. When in a hurry I might buy commercial ginger ale (I have to make a special trip across town to find real ginger ale) and grate fresh ginger into it. For myself, I make ginger tea many mornings and find it a refreshing morning drink that soothes and heals.

It certainly doesn't take a genius to realize that food affects our health. We know that if we drink too much we get a hangover, if we eat too much sugar we get hyperactive and then tired. It simply makes sense that other foods, especially herbs with their oils and compounds, can counter the effects of poor diet, help prevent cancer, diabetes, and other diseases, and stimulate the immune system. Over the past few years there has been a steady stream of scientific research proving folk medicine right.

So pick up a zester, a grater, and a good press and cook your way to better health. I hope you enjoy this book.

Notes on Cooking with Herbs

Most of the recipes in this book may be made with either fresh or dried herbs. Those that can only be made with fresh are noted. On the other hand, some recipes work better with dried herbs, and those are noted as well.

Buy dried herbs and spices in small quantities since they tend to lose their flavor after a time. Most lose significant flavor after about six months. Keep them away from heat and light, which affect the flavor.

You can increase the life of fresh herbs by storing them in the refrigerator with the stems in water or wrapped with a damp paper towel, and the tops covered with a plastic bag.

Notes on Ingredients

GARLIC   Nothing but fresh garlic is ever recommended. Jarred garlic or garlic flakes are not used, and neither are parsley flakes.

Garlic and parsley are readily available year-round; use no substitutions. That said, finding truly fresh garlic isn't always so easy. Supermarkets routinely sell garlic that has been on the shelf too long. Look for heads with tight, papery skin and firm cloves, be they purple or white. Spring is the best time to find great garlic.

GINGER   Fresh ginger and ground ginger are two different spices. Use only the spice called for, never substitute.

OIL   When specified, use extra-virgin olive oil. I always use this premium oil when making dressings or in any dish where the flavor of the oil is important. Extra-virgin olive oil has less than 1 percent acidity and comes from the first press of the olives. "Cold press" means the olives were crushed with granite stones (the only stone that will retain cold). "Pure" olive oil is made from a second or third pressing. For most sautéing or cooking you can use a less expensive olive oil.

Buy your olive oil in a can if you don't use a great deal. Light and warmth can cause olive oil to spoil more quickly, so it's a good idea to store your olive oils in a cool dark place.

For other vegetable oil, I use a canola or sunflower oil but often an olive oil will do just as well.

If using peanut, hazelnut, or walnut oil, use right away since these oils go bad quickly. Hazelnut and walnut oil are not good for cooking.

VINEGAR   Common wine vinegars (wine, cider, rice, and balsamic) are used throughout this book for dressings and sauces. Red wine vinegar is best suited for sauces and marinades, white for herb dressings and emulsions, rice for oriental cuisine, and balsamic for sauces and dressings. A good-quality vinegar (and quality is especially important with balsamic vinegar, which should come from Modena) will give your foods more depth.

PEPPERS Use care handling hot peppers. Serranos, poblanos, jalapeños, and others can burn when you try to seed them. Be sure to wash your hands well after handling, or use gloves.

To roast a pepper, first char it under a broiler, turning frequently, until blackened. Put it in a paper bag, close tightly, and let it steam itself for 20 minutes or so. The skin should then come off quickly and easily. Jars of roasted peppers are available in many grocery stores. Most hot peppers can be exchanged for others in recipes, so don't be disappointed if jalapeños are the only pepper you can find. If you are using a pepper which is hotter than the recommended one, simply use less.

TOMATOES To peel and seed tomatoes, drop into boiling water for about 15 seconds. Drain and peel. Cut the tomatoes in half crosswise and gently squeeze out the seeds.

YOGURT Used in these recipes is plain, nonfat, or lowfat as you prefer.

BROTH Low-salt chicken broth is recommended when using canned broth. If you use regular chicken broth, reduce or eliminate any salt called for in the recipe.

CHEESE Choose Parmesan cheese to grate yourself or freshly grated cheese from the deli section. That way you'll skip the preservatives in the packaged types and enjoy a much better tasting cheese.

I recommend lowfat or nonfat ricotta and cottage cheese in these recipes.

CURRY POWDER When you buy packaged curry powder, purchase a high-quality combination. Some discount and store brands may have an off taste due to inferior ingredients. Good ingredients yield the best results; it's worth the effort to find good powders in a specialty cookware shop or catalog, or make your own by using the mix presented in the Basic Recipes section of this book.

CHILE POWDER   As referred to in this book chile powder may be a blend of spices, or just ground dried chile peppers. As you would with curries, make sure you buy a quality chile powder for the best taste.

VEGETABLES   Don't overcook vegetables. The key to great flavor is slightly undercooked vegetables. Taste as you go is the best advice if you are unsure of the time.

BEANS   If you want to use dried black, red, or white beans rather than canned, soak them overnight in cold water, after first picking out any stones. (To quick-soak beans, cover with water and bring to a boil. Boil, covered, for a couple of minutes; remove from heat and let sit for at least an hour. Drain and use fresh water for cooking). I use both canned and fresh, depending upon the time I have available to make the dish.

SUBSTITUTES   When substituting, remember that some herbs have such a delicate flavor and taste that they should only be added at the end of a dish, just before it is served. Chervil, parsley, chives, salad burnet, savory, watercress, and marjoram generally lose their flavor over high heat. When substituting dried you will probably want to add the herb sooner than you would with fresh.

With many recipes you can freely substitute herbs that are close in flavor. If chives aren't available, use scallions. Substitute parsley for chervil or cilantro, and marjoram for oregano, or experiment with your own substitutions.

Cooking with Herbs

BEYOND CULINARY HERBS

This book focuses on culinary herbs and their uses. It's important for the reader to exercise caution and talk with a qualified herbalist, naturopath, or physician before using any herb for an extended period of time, or when other conditions exist in conjunction with the problem you want the herb to solve.

Please be even more cautious when pregnant.

Along with the culinary herbs in this book are some nonculinary herbs you may wish to explore for better health. These are common herbs, available at health food stores or from an herb store.

Burdock

FOR GOUT, COLDS, COUGHS   Burdock is a culinary herb used in soups in Japan and added to stews in Europe. The leaves may be added to salads as well. The flavor, in my opinion, does not enhance foods, so I have not included it in the recipes here.

Burdock leaf poultices have been used in both China and Europe to treat gout for centuries. In China the dried seedpod is also used for colds. It is also considered a good blood purifier.

Calendula

FOR BURNS, STINGS, VARICOSE VEINS, ULCERS   During the U.S. Civil War, calendula was used to treat wounds. The herb has a long medicinal history for many things from aches to ulcers, dating back to the Romans.

Today herbalists know calendula is especially good when used in a compress to heal burns and stings, and to help varicose veins. Calendula is useful for dry skin as well, and is sold in a cream form in many health stores.

The herb may have some value in helping stomach ailments, including ulcers, since it helps stimulate the flow of bile. Calendula should not be used during pregnancy.

Chamomile

FOR INSOMNIA   Chamomile calms the nerves and is gentle on the stomach. It contains volatile oils that help to soothe and calm, and herbalists have long recommended the herb for insomnia. The simplest way to enjoy chamomile is in tea.

Echinacea

FOR COLDS, FLU, AND THE IMMUNE SYSTEM   I first tried echinacea a few years ago at a friend's house and was assured a few drops of the strange-smelling mix would help fight off a flu. It did, and I have kept the herb in the medicine cabinet ever since.

In Europe the herb is prescribed by doctors to help the immune system and treat infections. Herbalists consider echinacea one of the best natural antibiotics. It is sold in liquid form in many herb and health stores.

Feverfew

FOR MIGRAINES   Feverfew was once thought to reduce fever, hence the name. Today feverfew is used to relieve the inflammation of arthritis and promote sleep. But its primary value is in fighting, and even preventing, migraine headaches. Research in the 1980s proved the herb's effectiveness, showing success against headaches about 70 percent of the time.

Ginseng

FOR STRESS, IMPOTENCY   Ginseng has had many outrageous claims made on its behalf, but science has shown the herb to be helpful in relieving stress by its positive effect on the adrenal cortex. Most herbalists today recommend the herb for those weakened by disease or stress, which follows ancient Chinese use of the herb. In China, however, ginseng is rarely used on its own, but is combined with other herbs. The Chinese also recommend the herb for impotence in men over 45.

Lavender

TO REJUVENATE   In France, children were often given lavender baths to protect their health. The herb's therapeutic uses are many, but most relate to soothing and rejuvenating the body. Herbalists recommend lavender to relieve stomach distress, stimulate the appetite, or as a remedy against insect bites and bruises. Its antibacterial actions are very good for healing cuts. Fresh lavender can be rubbed on the skin to deter insects as well.

Pennyroyal

FOR COLIC, COLDS, AND FLU   Pennyroyal is a member of the mint family, with a fragrance that is sharper and stronger than spearmint or peppermint. It has a very volatile oil which should never be used by pregnant women since it is an abortive.

Pennyroyal may be used sparingly in foods to replace mint. It is also a good repellent when rubbed on the skin, keeping away mosquitoes, flies, and other insects.

Raspberry Leaves

FOR MUSCLE SPASMS DURING PREGNANCY, CRAMPING Both Chinese and European herbalists have used the raspberry leaf for pregnant women. The leaves contain fragerine which is a relaxant that reduces muscle spasms in the uterus. In China, a cup of raspberry tea is recommended before meals. It is also used in Europe to help heavy cramping during menstruation.

Slippery Elm

FOR SORE THROATS, AS A LAXATIVE   Slippery elm bark is one of the safest and most gentle medicines. It is also a good source of calcium, easy to digest, and helpful to the stomach. In some parts of the U.S., slippery elm tea has been used as a laxative. Native Americans gave pregnant women a tea for labor, and used it as a poultice for fevers and burns. Slippery elm lozenges are available in health food stores and are effective for sore throats and congestion.

HERBS FOR AILMENTS

Here are some common ailments, and foods or herbs which contain compounds that may help with them.

ALLERGIES   onions, parsley. (Special note: Milk, despite the heavy advertising, may not be the healthful food you think it is, especially for children. Many scientists, doctors, herbalists, and naturopaths believe that milk actually triggers many allergies and even aches and pains. Milk allergies are common among children and may express themselves in something as simple as irritability. If you have problems with allergies, joint pain, irritable bowels, or asthma, try eliminating milk and dairy products.)

ANTI-CANCER   apples, asparagus, avocados, brussels sprouts, cabbage, carrots, cauliflower, celery, collard greens, corn, garlic (considered top potential cancer-preventive food by the National Cancer Institute), kale, kiwi, milk, mushrooms, nuts, onions, oranges, parsley, parsnips, potatoes, raspberries, rice, soybeans, spinach, strawberries, sweet potatoes (yams), tomatoes, watermelon, wheat bran.

Cooking with Herbs

APPETITE STIMULANT caraway seed, lavender, savory, tarragon.

APPETITE SUPPRESSION apples.

BLADDER/URINARY TRACT INFECTIONS cranberries.

BLOOD PRESSURE celery, fenugreek, fish, garlic.

BLOOD SUGAR beans, cinnamon, fenugreek, garlic, mustard, nuts, oats.

CHOLESTEROL REDUCTION apples, avocados, barley, beans, broccoli (best raw), carrots, fish, grapes, nuts (especially walnuts), oats, olive oil.

COLDS/FLU/CONGESTION bell pepper (extremely rich in vitamin C), borage, chile peppers, echinacea, eucalyptus, garlic, ginger, kiwi (vitamin C), lemon balm, mustard (vitamin C), onions, oranges (vitamin C), sage, slippery elm, soybeans, thyme, yogurt.

DEPRESSION basil, borage, brazil nuts, lemon balm, rosemary.

DIARRHEA blueberries, cinnamon, garlic, ginger.

DIURETICS celery, garlic, parsley.

DYSPEPSIA (upset stomach/nausea/indigestion) anise, bananas, chervil, coriander/cilantro, cumin, fennel, ginger, lemon verbena, marjoram, oregano, pineapple, rosemary.

FLATULENCE anise, coriander/cilantro, dill, fenugreek.

HEADACHES/MIGRAINES   corn, feverfew, ginger, rosemary.

HEART DISEASE   evening primrose, fish, garlic, grapes, rosemary, wine.

IMMUNE SYSTEM BOOSTERS   carrots, garlic, echinacea, ginseng, yogurt.

LAXATIVES   dates, plums, prunes.

STROKES   carrots.

ULCERS   broccoli (best raw), fenugreek.

BASIC RECIPES

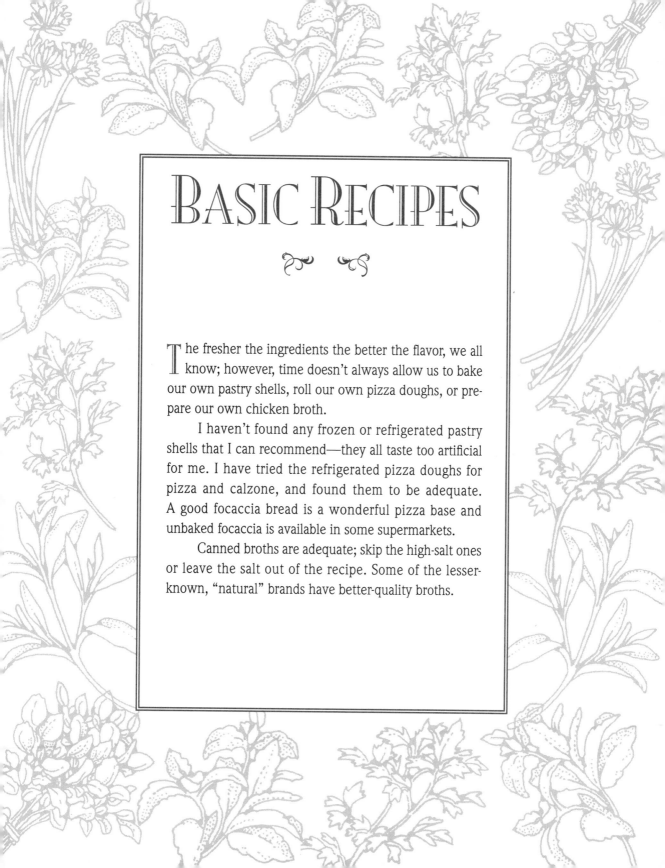

The fresher the ingredients the better the flavor, we all know; however, time doesn't always allow us to bake our own pastry shells, roll our own pizza doughs, or prepare our own chicken broth.

I haven't found any frozen or refrigerated pastry shells that I can recommend—they all taste too artificial for me. I have tried the refrigerated pizza doughs for pizza and calzone, and found them to be adequate. A good focaccia bread is a wonderful pizza base and unbaked focaccia is available in some supermarkets.

Canned broths are adequate; skip the high-salt ones or leave the salt out of the recipe. Some of the lesser-known, "natural" brands have better-quality broths.

Pizza Dough

૪૦ ৩૪

²⁄₃ cup warm water (110 to
115 degree)
1 package active dry yeast
(2½ teaspoons)
¼ teaspoon sugar
2 cups all-purpose flour
¼ teaspoon salt

PREPARATION TIME:
Less than 30 minutes
(plus 2 hours sitting time)

This is a pretty basic dough recipe. Don't forget you can use focaccia bread for pizza with good results.

Place water, yeast, and sugar in a mixing bowl. Stir, then let rest 5 minutes. Add flour and salt and mix with a dough hook for 3 minutes.

Place the dough in a large bowl, cover with plastic wrap, and set in a warm place for about 2 hours, or until the dough has doubled.

Makes 2 (9-inch) round crusts (2 servings)

467 Calories
14.2 g Protein
97.2 g Carbohydrates
1.3 g Fat
2% Calories from Fat
3.4 g Fiber
272 mg Sodium
0 mg Cholesterol

Cooking with Herbs

Pizza Sauce

֍֍ ֍֍

¼ cup extra-virgin olive oil
1 small onion, finely
    chopped
4 cloves garlic, minced
1 (28-ounce) can crushed
    tomatoes in juice
1 tablespoon dried dill
1 tablespoon dried thyme
2 bay leaves

PREPARATION TIME:
Less than 30 minutes

Bread machines and pre-cooked focaccia make good pizza at home a real possibility. Here's a simple, quick tomato sauce that is a winner with pizza or calzone—or tossed with pasta for that matter.

Place the oil, onion, and garlic in an unheated saucepan and stir to coat. Cook over moderate-low heat until garlic just begins to turn golden (but do not brown), 3 to 4 minutes. Add tomatoes and seasonings, bring to boil, reduce heat, and simmer 20 minutes. Discard bay leaves.

Makes about 2 cups (¹/₄ cup per serving)

92	Calories
1.4 g	Protein
6.9 g	Carbohydrates
7.0 g	Fat
68%	Calories from Fat
0.8 g	Fiber
263 mg	Sodium
0 mg	Cholesterol

Pie or Tart Shells

2½ tablespoons unsalted butter, cold
1 cup unbleached all-purpose flour
⅛ teaspoon salt
5 tablespoons ice water

PREPARATION TIME:
Less than 1 hour
(plus chilling time)

I haven't found particularly well prepared shells, so I use this recipe.

Cut butter into inch pieces. Combine flour, butter, and salt; mix until butter pieces are well coated with flour. Add half the water and, using two knives, cut through mixture to mix in water and cut up the butter pieces. Add remaining water over the dry parts of the dough, then cut in until all of the flour is damp. Roll dough into a ball and dust with flour. Wrap in plastic and refrigerate for 2 hours. Roll out the dough on a floured board into a 12-inch diameter. Place on a cookie sheet and chill at least 1 hour.

Makes 1 (9-inch) pie shell

93	Calories
1.7 g	Protein
12.4 g	Carbohydrates
3.9 g	Fat
38%	Calories from Fat
0.4 g	Fiber
34 mg	Sodium
10 mg	Cholesterol

Cooking with Herbs

Egg Noodles

꠸ ꠸

3 cups all-purpose flour,
    plus extra for dusting
4 large eggs, plus 1 egg
    yolk, at room
    temperature
1 teaspoon salt
2½ tablespoons extra-virgin
    olive oil
1 tablespoon warm water
2 tablespoons parsley or
    basil, minced
    (optional)

PREPARATION TIME:
Over 1 hour

These are great noodles for stews and, though quite a bit of work, they reward by just melting in your mouth.

Place the flour in a mixing bowl and make a large well in the center. Add the eggs, then salt, olive oil, water, and herbs. Slowly incorporate the eggs with the flour, a handful at a time. When all the flour is mixed, turn out onto a floured surface and knead until soft and smooth.

When soft, cover with plastic wrap and let sit for 30 minutes. Remove the wrap and cut the dough into six pieces. Cover five while you work with one piece, rolling the dough out. The dough needs to dry slightly, about 2 to 6 minutes, before cutting. It should no longer be sticky, but should not be brittle. Coil the dough and cut to desired thickness, then uncoil each strand and dry on a pasta rack. The pasta should dry for 2 hours before cooking. If cooking before 2 hours, cook in boiling water for just seconds. If dried for 2 hours or a full day, they will take 1 to 3 minutes to cook.

Makes about 1³⁄₄ pounds (6 to 8 servings)

255	Calories
8.4 g	Protein
36.6 g	Carbohydrates
7.8 g	Fat
27%	Calories from Fat
1.3 g	Fiber
300 mg	Sodium
134 mg	Cholesterol

Vegetable Broth

2 large onions, coarsely
   chopped
3 stalks celery, coarsely
   chopped
1 white turnip, peeled and
   coarsely chopped
1 whole garlic bulb,
   unpeeled, quartered
1 bunch parsley
10 carrots, coarsely chopped
3 cups lettuce, chopped
2 teaspoons fresh thyme, or
   $\frac{1}{2}$ teaspoon dried
2 teaspoons fresh marjoram,
   or $\frac{1}{2}$ teaspoon dried
2 teaspoons pepper
4 quarts water

PREPARATION TIME:
Over 1 hour

Canned vegetable broth is no match for homemade. Here's a simple recipe to make your own.

Place all vegetables and spices in a large pot and add water. Bring to a boil, then lower heat and simmer, partially covered, until vegetables become soft (about an hour). Pour soup through a colander, pressing the vegetables to extract juices. Discard solids. Pour broth through cheesecloth or a strainer. Cool before refrigerating.

Makes about 3 quarts (1 cup per serving)

10	Calories
0.5 g	Protein
1.8 g	Carbohydrates
0.1 g	Fat
9%	Calories from Fat
0.0 g	Fiber
4 mg	Sodium
0 mg	Cholesterol

Cooking with Herbs

Basic Mexican Salsa

4 fresh tomatillos
4 tomatoes, peeled, seeded, and chopped
2 jalapeños, seeded and minced
3 cloves garlic, minced
1 sweet onion, chopped
½ cup chopped fresh cilantro
1 tablespoon extra-virgin olive oil
1 tablespoon lemon juice
⅛ teaspoon ground cumin
⅛ teaspoon salt
⅛ teaspoon pepper

PREPARATION TIME:
Less than 30 minutes

This is great stuff, and so much better when fresh. Add or delete hot peppers to taste.

Remove the papery husk and boil tomatillos in water to cover, 3 to 4 minutes, watching carefully to make sure they remain firm. Drain and chop, then combine with remaining ingredients and toss. Chill before serving.

Makes about 6 cups (2 tablespoons per serving)

7	Calories
0.2 g	Protein
1.1 g	Carbohydrates
0.3 g	Fat
42%	Calories from Fat
0.3 g	Fiber
27 mg	Sodium
0 mg	Cholesterol

Basic Herb Vinaigrette

½ cup extra-virgin olive oil
¼ cup balsamic vinegar
3 tablespoons lemon juice
1 clove garlic, minced
½ teaspoon fresh chopped
    herbs (rosemary,
    tarragon, parsley)
⅛ teaspoon salt
⅛ teaspoon pepper

PREPARATION TIME:
Less than 30 minutes

Dressings are simply a mixture of fat and acid, usually oil and vinegar, mixed at 2 or 3 to 1. If desired, modify this dressing by adding a little Dijon mustard. With this basic mix you can make any vinaigrette you desire. Remember to use mild herbs more generously, and taste as you go with strong herbs such as oregano.

Whisk all together.

Makes about 1 cup (2 tablespoons per serving)

130	Calories
0.1 g	Protein
2.7 g	Carbohydrates
13.5 g	Fat
93%	Calories from Fat
0.0 g	Fiber
35 mg	Sodium
0 mg	Cholesterol

Cooking with Herbs

Curry Powder

1 teaspoon cayenne
    (or hotter to taste)
2 teaspoons cumin
8 teaspoons ground
    cardamom
8 teaspoons ground
    coriander
4 teaspoons turmeric
8 teaspoons paprika
2 teaspoons cinnamon
1 teaspoon mace
2 teaspoons fenugreek
1 teaspoon kosher salt

PREPARATION TIME:
Less than 30 minutes

I mix my own curry powder, using fresh spices. I do not include ground ginger, because I prefer fresh ginger in my recipes. Grind the seeds for the best flavor, or buy in small quantities in bulk from a specialty store. This curry is a little sweeter than many. You can spice it up by adding more cayenne, if desired.

Combine all ingredients. Store in a sealed jar in a cool, dark place.

Makes ³/₄ cup

Nutritional analysis reflects contents in 1 teaspoon

7	Calories
0.3 g	Protein
1.3 g	Carbohydrates
0.3 g	Fat
34%	Calories from Fat
0.3 g	Fiber
55 mg	Sodium
0 mg	Cholesterol

ANISE

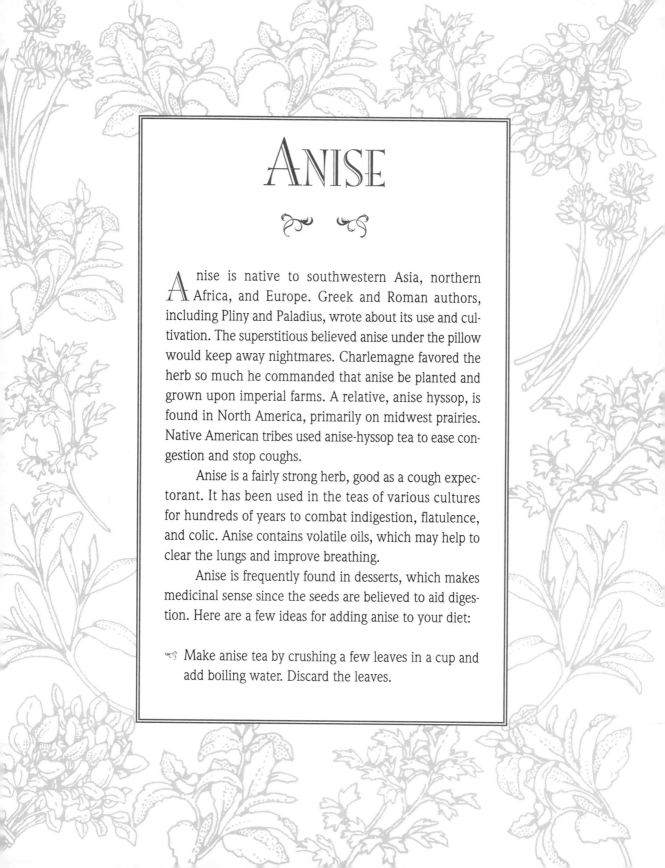

Anise is native to southwestern Asia, northern Africa, and Europe. Greek and Roman authors, including Pliny and Paladius, wrote about its use and cultivation. The superstitious believed anise under the pillow would keep away nightmares. Charlemagne favored the herb so much he commanded that anise be planted and grown upon imperial farms. A relative, anise hyssop, is found in North America, primarily on midwest prairies. Native American tribes used anise-hyssop tea to ease congestion and stop coughs.

Anise is a fairly strong herb, good as a cough expectorant. It has been used in the teas of various cultures for hundreds of years to combat indigestion, flatulence, and colic. Anise contains volatile oils, which may help to clear the lungs and improve breathing.

Anise is frequently found in desserts, which makes medicinal sense since the seeds are believed to aid digestion. Here are a few ideas for adding anise to your diet:

- Make anise tea by crushing a few leaves in a cup and add boiling water. Discard the leaves.

- Anise-hyssop tea, also made with the leaves, is sweet enough to replace some or all of the sugar in recipes. Use the tea to flavor vegetable salads, shellfish, and fruit salad recipes, or use a little to flavor a bottle of cold water.
- Add anise seed to your curry powder.
- Use a teaspoon of anise seed in your favorite bread recipe.
- Stir a little anise seed into cheeses, including cottage cheese.
- Sprinkle a vegetable appetizer with anise seed.
- Add ground anise seed as a replacement for cinnamon in cookie recipes.
- Sprinkle ground anise seed over a plate of apples and pears.
- Use the seed to add sweetness to vegetable and meat stews.
- Use $\frac{1}{4}$ teaspoon anise seed in a fruit pie.
- Top rolls and coffee cakes with a light sprinkling of ground anise seeds.

Herb Bread

❦ ❧

2 tablespoons yeast
5 tablespoons sugar
1½ cups warm water
2 eggs
⅓ cup vegetable oil
2 teaspoons dill
1 teaspoon anise seed
¼ cup chopped parsley
2 teaspoons salt
7 cups flour
1 cup finely chopped onion

PREPARATION TIME:
Over 1 hour

This wonderful bread is great with a soup in the winter, or with a salad in summer. It will aid digestion with its anise and parsley.

Dissolve the yeast and sugar in warm water. Stir, then let sit for 5 minutes. Meanwhile, combine the eggs, oil, dill, anise, parsley, and salt in a large mixing bowl. When the yeast mixture is bubbling, add to the large bowl.

Gradually whisk in 3 cups of the flour and beat 5 to 6 minutes, scraping down the sides as needed. Add chopped onion and stir with a spoon. Add 3 more cups of flour, making certain that each cup of flour is absorbed before repeating with another cup.

Turn out the dough onto a lightly floured board and knead, using remaining flour as needed. Knead 6 or 7 minutes. Place dough into an oiled bowl. Oil top of dough slightly, then cover with plastic wrap and a dish towel. Store in a warm place to double in size, about 2 hours. Knead again briefly to remove air bubbles, divide in half, and form two loaves. Place in two bread pans, cover again with a towel, and let rise until doubled again, about 90 minutes. Bake at 375 degrees for 30 minutes.

Makes 2 loaves (32 slices)

137 Calories
3.5 g Protein
23.8 g Carbohydrates
3.0 g Fat
19% Calories from Fat
0.9 g Fiber
138 mg Sodium
13 mg Cholesterol

Chicken or Vegetarian Pie with Cilantro and Anise Seed Cheese Crust

෨ ෬

Pie Crust

1 cup unbleached
all-purpose flour
2½ tablespoons unsalted
butter, cold
⅛ teaspoon salt
¼ teaspoon ground anise
seed
5 tablespoons ice water

Filling

2 tablespoons extra-virgin
olive oil
1 onion, chopped
4 mushrooms, sliced
½ bell pepper, diced
3 tablespoons flour
½ cup peas, fresh or frozen
½ cup corn, fresh or frozen
1 boneless, skinless
chicken breast,
cooked and shredded
(or chopped)
1½ cups vegetable broth or
water
½ teaspoon dried oregano
½ teaspoon dried thyme
¼ cup fresh chopped
cilantro
¼ teaspoon salt
¼ teaspoon pepper

PREPARATION TIME:
Over 1 hour

The anise in the crust goes wonderfully with a rich pot pie. Vegetarians can replace the chicken with half of an eggplant, diced. Sauté the eggplant with the mushrooms and peppers.

Cut butter into inch-long pieces. Combine flour, butter, and salt; mix until butter pieces are well coated with flour. Add anise seed and half the water and, using two knives, cut through mixture to mix in water and cut up the butter pieces. Add the remaining water over the dry parts of the dough, then cut in until all of the flour is damp. Roll dough into a ball and dust with flour. Wrap in plastic and refrigerate for 2 hours. Roll dough onto a floured board to a 12-inch diameter. Place on a cookie sheet and chill at least 1 hour.

Preheat oven to 400 degrees. Heat oil and sauté the onion, mushrooms, and pepper until soft, about 8 minutes. Add flour and mix well, then stir in the remaining ingredients and remove from heat. Place the piecrust in a lightly oiled baking dish and spoon vegetable mixture into the pie. Prick with a fork to vent. Bake 25 minutes.

Serves 6

263	Calories
13.3 g	Protein
27.4 g	Carbohydrates
11.1 g	Fat
41%	Calories from Fat
2.0 g	Fiber
170 mg	Sodium
38 mg	Cholesterol

Cooking with Herbs

Vegetable Stew with Anise and Cilantro

❧ ❧

2 small onions, chopped
1 bell pepper, chopped
3 tablespoons olive oil
½ teaspoon ground anise
 seed
1 teaspoon dried
 marjoram
1½ cups fresh green beans,
 1-inch pieces (thawed
 if frozen)
1 (28-ounce) can tomatoes
 (or 3 cups fresh,
 peeled with juice)
1 zucchini or yellow
 squash, sliced
2 tablespoons (or more)
 fresh chopped cilantro

PREPARATION TIME:
Less than 1 hour

Easy to make, and it is a meal when served with bread. Anise has an inspiring effect on the vegetables in this dish.

Sauté onions and pepper in olive oil about 5 minutes, until onions begin to soften. Add spices and green beans and sauté another 3 to 4 minutes. Add tomatoes and zucchini, cover, and simmer 15 to 20 minutes, until vegetables are tender. Serve in bowls and sprinkle with chopped coriander.

Serves 4 to 6

131	Calories
3.2 g	Protein
15.4 g	Carbohydrates
7.3 g	Fat
50%	Calories from Fat
2.8 g	Fiber
351 mg	Sodium
0 mg	Cholesterol

Quick Sweet and Sour Chicken

¼ cup catsup
⅛ cup soy sauce
⅓ cup cider vinegar
⅓ cup brown sugar
¼ teaspoon anise seed
¾ cup water
1 tablespoon cornstarch,
    dissolved in 2 table-
    spoons of water
2 boneless, skinless chicken
    breasts

PREPARATION TIME:
Less than 30 minutes

Use this sweet and sour with stir-fry, over rice, on vegetables, or cook chicken pieces in the sauce.

Mix the first six ingredients together in a small bowl. Whisk in the dissolved cornstarch. Place the sauce in a skillet and warm. Place the chicken in the sauce and sauté 4 to 5 minutes on one side. Turn and cook another 3 to 4 minutes, or until done (be careful not to overcook).

Serves 4

246	Calories
27.4 g	Protein
26.6 g	Carbohydrates
3.1 g	Fat
11%	Calories from Fat
0.3 g	Fiber
765 mg	Sodium
73 mg	Cholesterol

Cooking with Herbs

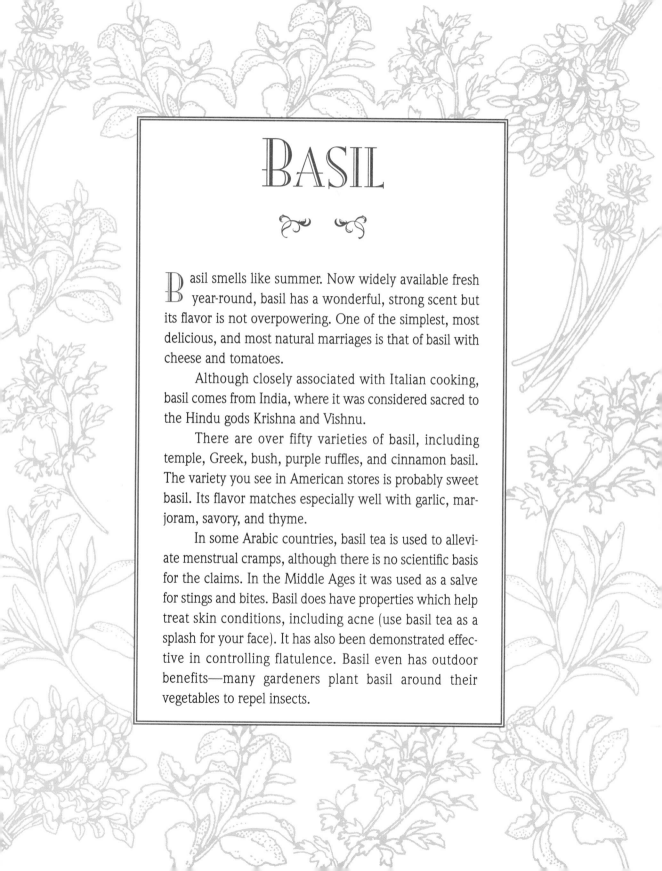

BASIL

Basil smells like summer. Now widely available fresh year-round, basil has a wonderful, strong scent but its flavor is not overpowering. One of the simplest, most delicious, and most natural marriages is that of basil with cheese and tomatoes.

Although closely associated with Italian cooking, basil comes from India, where it was considered sacred to the Hindu gods Krishna and Vishnu.

There are over fifty varieties of basil, including temple, Greek, bush, purple ruffles, and cinnamon basil. The variety you see in American stores is probably sweet basil. Its flavor matches especially well with garlic, marjoram, savory, and thyme.

In some Arabic countries, basil tea is used to alleviate menstrual cramps, although there is no scientific basis for the claims. In the Middle Ages it was used as a salve for stings and bites. Basil does have properties which help treat skin conditions, including acne (use basil tea as a splash for your face). It has also been demonstrated effective in controlling flatulence. Basil even has outdoor benefits—many gardeners plant basil around their vegetables to repel insects.

Some health professionals recommend basil tea as a mood enhancer and to combat the effects of chemotherapy, although the flavor of basil tea is too strong for most people to enjoy.

Fresh basil is very flexible, which is important for an herb that doesn't last long in the refrigerator. Here are some ideas for basil:

- Add fresh basil to an omelet or scrambled eggs.
- Mix into butter and serve over rice or with fish, especially fresh tuna.
- Add fresh or dried basil to vegetable and cream soups.
- Sprinkle fresh basil over cooked vegetables, including asparagus and zucchini.
- Mix into a vinaigrette.
- Basil goes well in many sauces. Fresh basil is a must for spaghetti sauce, of course, but is also good in many cream sauces.
- Add fresh basil to simple pasta dishes.
- Mix fresh basil into salads.
- Serve a basil leaf atop a slice of tomato and a slice of mozzarella—a wonderful appetizer.
- Add a basil leaf to a glass of iced tea.

Cooking with Herbs

Basil Tea

½ cup basil leaves, crushed
2½ cups water
2 teabags (orange pekoe)
½ inch fresh ginger, sliced
1 teaspoon honey,
   or to taste

PREPARATION TIME:
Less than 15 minutes

This is strong tea. You can also use it as a splash to help your skin.

Boil basil in water for 3 to 4 minutes, then add teabags and ginger and simmer another 2 minutes. Remove from heat and steep for 5 minutes. Strain and serve.

Serves 2

14	Calories
0.0 g	Protein
3.4 g	Carbohydrates
0.0 g	Fat
0%	Calories from Fat
0.0 g	Fiber
6 mg	Sodium
0 mg	Cholesterol

Warm Pasta and Basil Salad

⤳ ⤺

1 pound farfalle (bowtie) or
   other pasta
3 to 4 cherry tomatoes,
   halved
½ sweet onion, halved and
   thinly sliced
1 red bell pepper, seeded
   and thinly sliced
½ cup calamata olives, pits
   removed and cut
   in half
2 tablespoons fresh
   chopped basil
2 teaspoons lemon zest
2 tablespoons parsley
6 tablespoons olive oil
3 tablespoons lemon juice
½ cup crumbled feta cheese

PREPARATION TIME:
Less than 30 minutes

This makes a nice easy lunch, or a good side dish with a barbecue.

Cook pasta according to package instructions. Meanwhile, combine tomatoes, onion, bell pepper, and olives in a bowl. In a small bowl, combine remaining ingredients, except the cheese, and toss with vegetables. Add cooked pasta and mix well. Sprinkle feta cheese on top. Serve warm or at room temperature.

Serves 4 as a main dish, 6 as a side dish

470	Calories
11.0 g	Protein
58.2 g	Carbohydrates
22.0 g	Fat
42%	Calories from Fat
5.8 g	Fiber
575 mg	Sodium
8 mg	Cholesterol

Cooking with Herbs

Bowtie Salad with Herbs and Lemon

1 pound farfalle (bowtie) or other pasta

2 tablespoons extra-virgin olive oil

12 (or more) cherry tomatoes, halved

2 cups fresh chopped spinach

½ cup fresh chopped basil

¼ cup herb mix, such as chives, thyme, tarragon, parsley

2 tablespoons lemon zest

3 tablespoons strong-flavored herbs, such as oregano, savory, rosemary, or marjoram

3 tablespoons lemon juice

PREPARATION TIME:
Less than 30 minutes

Mix and match the herbs you like for this pasta salad, cutting back on the basil and increasing other herbs if desired.

Cook pasta according to package directions, drain, and rinse well under cold water. Toss with olive oil to coat, then toss again with remaining ingredients. Serve at room temperature or slightly chilled.

Serves 4

487	Calories
15.3 g	Protein
86.8 g	Carbohydrates
9.1 g	Fat
16%	Calories from Fat
9.7 g	Fiber
33 mg	Sodium
0 mg	Cholesterol

Mediterranean Fish and Pasta

༝ ༝

1 pound penne or other
    hollow pasta
1 tablespoon plus $\frac{1}{4}$ cup
    extra-virgin olive oil
3 cloves garlic, minced
8 roma tomatoes, halved
    and sliced
$\frac{1}{4}$ cup fresh chopped basil
1 teaspoon fresh thyme, or
    $\frac{1}{2}$ teaspoon dried
$\frac{3}{4}$ cup dry white wine
4 tablespoons lemon juice
1 pound sole, cut into short
    strips
$\frac{1}{2}$ cup calamata olives,
    pitted and halved

PREPARATION TIME:
Less than 1 hour

This easy dish has both Greek and Italian flavors. It is a wonderful dish for company.

Cook pasta according to package directions, drain, and toss with the tablespoon of olive oil. Set aside. In a large skillet heat $\frac{1}{4}$ cup olive oil. Add garlic and sauté over low heat 5 minutes. Add tomatoes, basil, thyme, wine, and lemon juice and cook over medium high heat for another 5 minutes. Add remaining ingredients and cook until fish is cooked, about 3 minutes. Add cooked pasta and toss well.

Serves 4 to 6

499	Calories
24.1 g	Protein
59.1 g	Carbohydrates
17.0 g	Fat
30%	Calories from Fat
6.2 g	Fiber
381 mg	Sodium
36 mg	Cholesterol

Cooking with Herbs

Green Rice

❧ ❧

¼ cup fresh chopped basil
½ cup fresh chopped
    cilantro
2 tablespoons chopped
    green onions
3 to 4 tablespoons olive oil
2½ cups warm cooked rice
    (1 cup uncooked)

PREPARATION TIME:
Less than 30 minutes

A mixture of two green herbs gives rice the definite color of green. Add a chopped red pepper if you like.

Place basil, cilantro, and onions in blender or food processor with about half the oil. Purée, adding additional oil as necessary. Stir into cooked rice.

Serves 4

258	Calories
3.7 g	Protein
36.5 g	Carbohydrates
10.5 g	Fat
36%	Calories from Fat
0.9 g	Fiber
8 mg	Sodium
0 mg	Cholesterol

Red Pepper and Basil Pizza

~ ~

3 cups seeded, cored, roasted red bell peppers
1 (16-ounce) can tomatoes, drained
1 clove garlic, minced
1 scallion, minced
$\frac{1}{3}$ cup extra-virgin olive oil
$\frac{1}{2}$ teaspoon fresh chopped oregano, or $\frac{1}{4}$ teaspoon dried
1 tablespoon red wine vinegar
$\frac{1}{4}$ cup fresh chopped basil
$\frac{1}{2}$ teaspoon salt
$\frac{1}{4}$ teaspoon pepper
1 large focaccia bread or prepared pizza crust
Mozzarella cheese and other toppings of your choice (optional)

PREPARATION TIME:
Less than 1 hour

This is great on pizza, grated with mozzarella and the toppings you choose. Try it with pasta as well.

Place peppers, tomatoes, garlic, and scallion in a food processor and blend until smooth. Pour into a saucepan with the olive oil and oregano, and simmer 15 to 20 minutes, or until thickened, stirring occasionally. Pour in vinegar, and stir in basil, salt, and pepper. Spread sauce on the focaccia bread or pizza crust, and top with cheese or any other pizza toppings you desire; heat 10 to 15 minutes, or until hot and bubbly.

Makes enough sauce for 1 or 2 pizzas

1035	Calories
30.6 g	Protein
124.9 g	Carbohydrates
50.9 g	Fat
44%	Calories from Fat
7.2 g	Fiber
2371 mg	Sodium
10 mg	Cholesterol

Cooking with Herbs

Penne with No-Cook Basil Sauce

12 ounces penne or other
   hollow pasta
 3 to 4 fresh tomatoes,
   peeled and quartered
½ cup fresh basil leaves
 2 teaspoons fresh oregano,
   or 1 teaspoon dried
 2 cloves garlic, chopped or
   minced
 1 tablespoon extra-virgin
   olive oil
   Additional basil for
   garnish

PREPARATION TIME:
Less than 30 minutes

This dish must be made with fresh basil and is best when made with fresh oregano as well.

Cook pasta according to package directions. Place remaining ingredients in a blender and purée. Toss the sauce with the pasta, then sprinkle with chopped basil garnish.

Serves 4

349	Calories
11.1 g	Protein
64.8 g	Carbohydrates
5.1 g	Fat
13%	Calories from Fat
7.1 g	Fiber
10 mg	Sodium
0 mg	Cholesterol

Lemon Basil Ravioli

❧ ❧

Zest of 1 lemon
1 tablespoon lemon juice
1½ cups fresh basil leaves
½ cup walnuts
1 cup ricotta cheese
¼ cup grated Parmesan
Ravioli dough or
won ton wrappers

PREPARATION TIME:
Less than 1 hour

This ravioli is good with a simple drizzle of olive oil or butter, or add a little lemon zest to an Alfredo style sauce.

Combine first six ingredients in a processor or blender and chop, then stuff into ravioli or won ton. Bring a pot of water to a boil, then cook ravioli for 2 minutes, or until they float to the surface.

Serves 4

324	Calories
16.7 g	Protein
42.0 g	Carbohydrates
11.2 g	Fat
31%	Calories from Fat
2.0 g	Fiber
249 mg	Sodium
23 mg	Cholesterol

Red Pepper Relish

3 red peppers, roasted and chopped into small pieces

2 tablespoons fresh basil, minced

1 tablespoon parsley, minced

1 teaspoon fresh oregano, minced

2 tablespoons balsamic vinegar

1 tablespoon fresh lemon juice

3 tablespoons extra-virgin olive oil

1 teaspoon pepper

PREPARATION TIME:
Less than 30 minutes
(plus standing time)

The roasted peppers go well with the herbs. I use this as a condiment for cold meats or vegetables.

Combine all ingredients together, cover, and let sit for at least 30 minutes.

Makes about 2$^1/_2$ cups (1 tablespoon per serving)

12	Calories
0.1 g	Protein
0.5 g	Carbohydrates
1.1 g	Fat
83%	Calories from Fat
0.1 g	Fiber
23 mg	Sodium
0 mg	Cholesterol

BAY LEAF

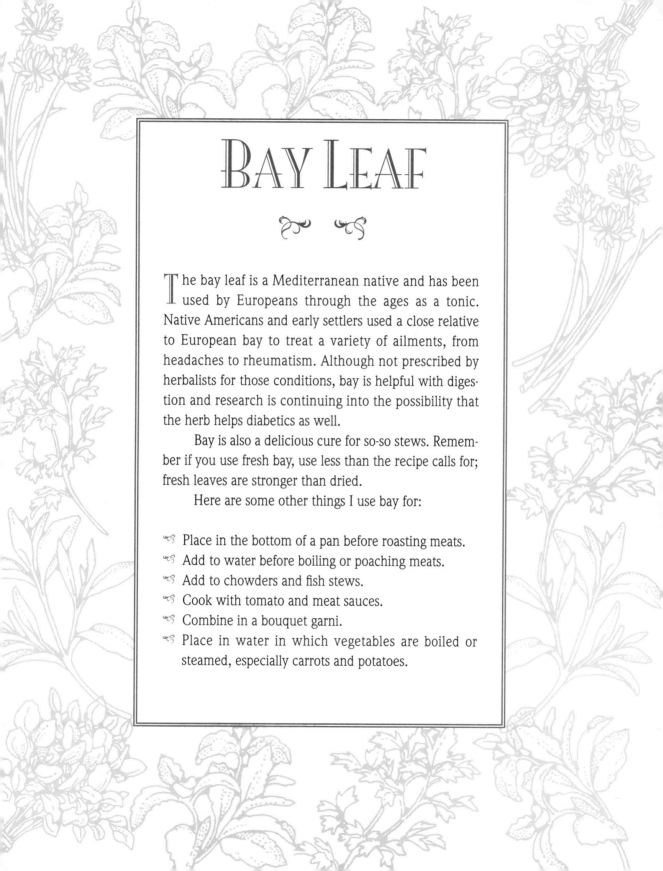

The bay leaf is a Mediterranean native and has been used by Europeans through the ages as a tonic. Native Americans and early settlers used a close relative to European bay to treat a variety of ailments, from headaches to rheumatism. Although not prescribed by herbalists for those conditions, bay is helpful with digestion and research is continuing into the possibility that the herb helps diabetics as well.

Bay is also a delicious cure for so-so stews. Remember if you use fresh bay, use less than the recipe calls for; fresh leaves are stronger than dried.

Here are some other things I use bay for:

- Place in the bottom of a pan before roasting meats.
- Add to water before boiling or poaching meats.
- Add to chowders and fish stews.
- Cook with tomato and meat sauces.
- Combine in a bouquet garni.
- Place in water in which vegetables are boiled or steamed, especially carrots and potatoes.

Tomato Bisque

1 tablespoon butter
1 onion, chopped
2 cups whole tomatoes, peeled chopped with juice, or 1 (28-ounce) can
2 tablespoons honey
1 bay leaf
$\frac{1}{2}$ teaspoon allspice
1 teaspoon dried marjoram
$\frac{1}{4}$ teaspoon pepper
1 cup evaporated skim milk
4 tablespoons milk
2 tablespoons cornstarch

PREPARATION TIME:
Less than 30 minutes

This is a soup children seem to love. It's easy to make and very warming in cold weather.

Melt butter and sauté onion until soft, about 7 minutes. Add tomatoes, honey, bay leaf, allspice, marjoram, and pepper and simmer 7 minutes. Meanwhile, heat the evaporated milk in a saucepan but do not boil. Dissolve cornstarch in milk, then whisk into the evaporated milk. Cook, stirring constantly, until thick, about 2 minutes. Add tomato mixture to the milk, very slowly to prevent curdling. Remove bay leaf. Heat, but do not boil.

Serves 4

192	Calories
7.8 g	Protein
33.0 g	Carbohydrates
3.9 g	Fat
18%	Calories from Fat
1.6 g	Fiber
633 mg	Sodium
12 mg	Cholesterol

Cooking with Herbs

Halibut Casserole

෴ ෴

4 small halibut fillets
1 tablespoon lemon juice
¼ cup extra-virgin olive oil
½ onion, chopped
½ green pepper, finely
    chopped
2 cloves garlic, minced
3 bay leaves
2 tomatoes, peeled,
    seeded, and finely
    chopped
¼ cup chopped parsley
⅓ cup dry white wine
1 teaspoon pepper
3 potatoes, peeled and
    quartered
1 tomato, thinly sliced
    (optional)

PREPARATION TIME:
Less than 1 hour

*Substitute red snapper or mackerel for the halibut, if you like.
This is a dish with Mediterranean flavors.*

Place fish in a baking pan and sprinkle with lemon juice. Preheat
oven to 325 degrees. Heat olive oil in a skillet and sauté onion,
pepper, and garlic 7 minutes, until soft. Add bay leaves, tomatoes, parsley, wine, and pepper and stir. Cook 15 minutes,
until thickened, stirring occasionally. Remove bay leaves. Pour
tomato mixture over fish, then arrange potatoes in the pan
around the fish. Place tomato slices on top if you desire and bake
25 minutes.

Serves 4

464	Calories
45.3 g	Protein
26.9 g	Carbohydrates
18.6 g	Fat
36%	Calories from Fat
3.0 g	Fiber
124 mg	Sodium
65 mg	Cholesterol

Herb Marinade for Fish

½ cup extra-virgin olive oil
2 bay leaves, crumbled
1 clove garlic, minced
1 tablespoon minced
   rosemary
1 tablespoon minced
   marjoram
2 tablespoons minced
   basil
½ teaspoon pepper
1½ pounds fish

PREPARATION TIME:
Less than 30 minutes
(plus marinating time)

This is a simple Mediterranean marinade, one you can use with cod, perch, red snapper, bass, and other fish. Substitute whatever fresh herbs you have on hand for the ones listed here.

Combine all ingredients and pour over the fish. Marinate 30 minutes or longer.

Makes enough for up to 2 pounds of fish (4 servings)

324	Calories
44.1 g	Protein
0.5 g	Carbohydrates
15.2 g	Fat
42%	Calories from Fat
0.1 g	Fiber
151 mg	Sodium
106 mg	Cholesterol

Simple Fish Stew

৵ ৵

2 tablespoons olive oil
2 onions, diced
5 cloves garlic, minced
½ teaspoon fennel seeds
⅛ teaspoon allspice
¼ teaspoon salt
¼ teaspoon pepper
2 cups peeled, seeded,
    and chopped
    tomatoes, or
    1 (28-ounce) can,
    drained
3 large potatoes, peeled
    and cut into large
    dice
2 bay leaves
1 tablespoon lemon zest
1½ pounds cod, cut into
    chunks
1½ tablespoons lemon juice

PREPARATION TIME:
Less than 1 hour

This hearty stew is great served with bread.

Heat oil and sauté onion and garlic until very soft, about 15 minutes. Add fennel, allspice, salt, and pepper and mix well for 2 minutes. Add tomatoes, potatoes, bay leaf, zest, and about 2 cups of water and simmer, partially covered, until the vegetables are soft, about 25 minutes. Add the fish and cook until done, about 5 minutes. Stir in lemon juice.

Serves 6 to 8

200	Calories
18.1 g	Protein
22.7 g	Carbohydrates
4.3 g	Fat
19%	Calories from Fat
2.2 g	Fiber
379 mg	Sodium
37 mg	Cholesterol

BORAGE

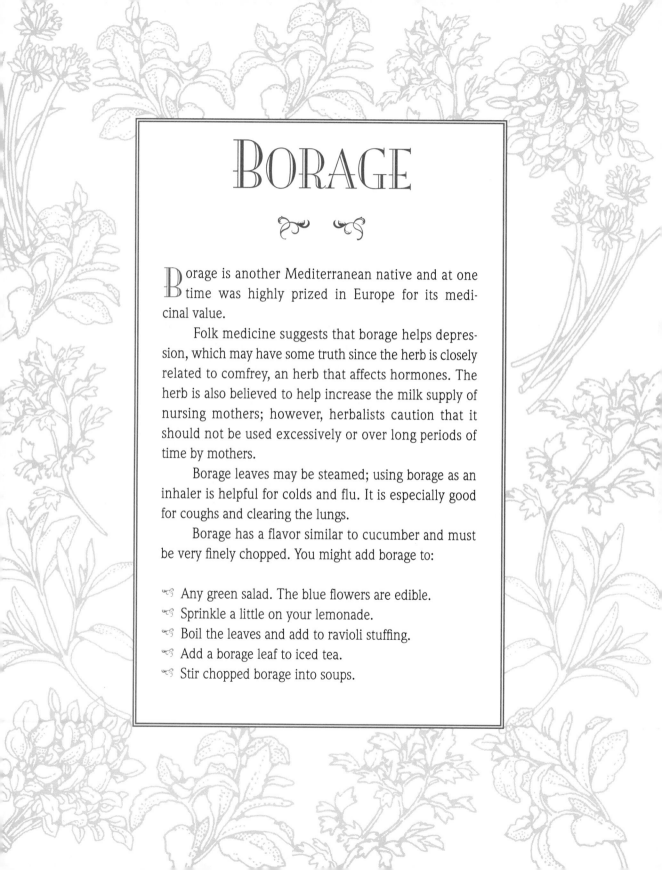

Borage is another Mediterranean native and at one time was highly prized in Europe for its medicinal value.

Folk medicine suggests that borage helps depression, which may have some truth since the herb is closely related to comfrey, an herb that affects hormones. The herb is also believed to help increase the milk supply of nursing mothers; however, herbalists caution that it should not be used excessively or over long periods of time by mothers.

Borage leaves may be steamed; using borage as an inhaler is helpful for colds and flu. It is especially good for coughs and clearing the lungs.

Borage has a flavor similar to cucumber and must be very finely chopped. You might add borage to:

- Any green salad. The blue flowers are edible.
- Sprinkle a little on your lemonade.
- Boil the leaves and add to ravioli stuffing.
- Add a borage leaf to iced tea.
- Stir chopped borage into soups.

Cold Apple and Buttermilk Soup with Borage

⁊⌀ ⍺⌀

1 tablespoon butter
1 cup chopped onion
2 large apples, peeled,
    cored, and diced
1 cup chicken broth
1¼ cups water
1¼ cups buttermilk
¼ cup cream, half-and-half,
    or plain yogurt
2 tablespoons lemon juice
1 cucumber, peeled,
    seeded, and diced
¾ cup corn, cooked
1 tablespoon borage,
    finely minced

PREPARATION TIME:
Less than 1 hour
(plus chilling time)

This is a delicious cold soup. If borage is unavailable, try lemon verbena or even parsley.

Sauté onion in butter until soft, about 10 minutes. Add apples, broth, and water, and bring to a boil; reduce heat and simmer 10 minutes, or until apples are tender. Remove from heat and cool to room temperature.

Purée the mixture in batches in a blender or food processor. Transfer to a bowl and stir in the buttermilk, cream, lemon juice, cucumber, and corn. Cover and chill for at least 2 hours. Sprinkle with borage before serving.

Serves 4 to 6

119	Calories
3.7 g	Protein
19.2 g	Carbohydrates
4.0 g	Fat
30%	Calories from Fat
2.4 g	Fiber
97 mg	Sodium
11 mg	Cholesterol

Cooking with Herbs

Green Beans and Tomatoes with Borage

☞ ☜

1 pound green beans
1 onion, cut in half and
  thinly sliced
3 tomatoes, halved and
  thinly sliced
⅓ cup extra-virgin olive oil
4 tablespoons red wine
  vinegar
1 teaspoon chopped borage
¼ teaspoon dried thyme
⅛ teaspoon salt
⅛ teaspoon pepper

PREPARATION TIME:
Less than 30 minutes

This is an easy side dish. If you don't have borage, use a little parsley.

Steam or boil the beans until just tender, about 5 minutes. Combine with onion and tomatoes. Combine remaining ingredients and mix well, then toss with beans and onion.

Serves 4 to 6

158	Calories
2.3 g	Protein
11.8 g	Carbohydrates
12.5 g	Fat
71%	Calories from Fat
2.6 g	Fiber
52 mg	Sodium
0 mg	Cholesterol

CARAWAY SEED

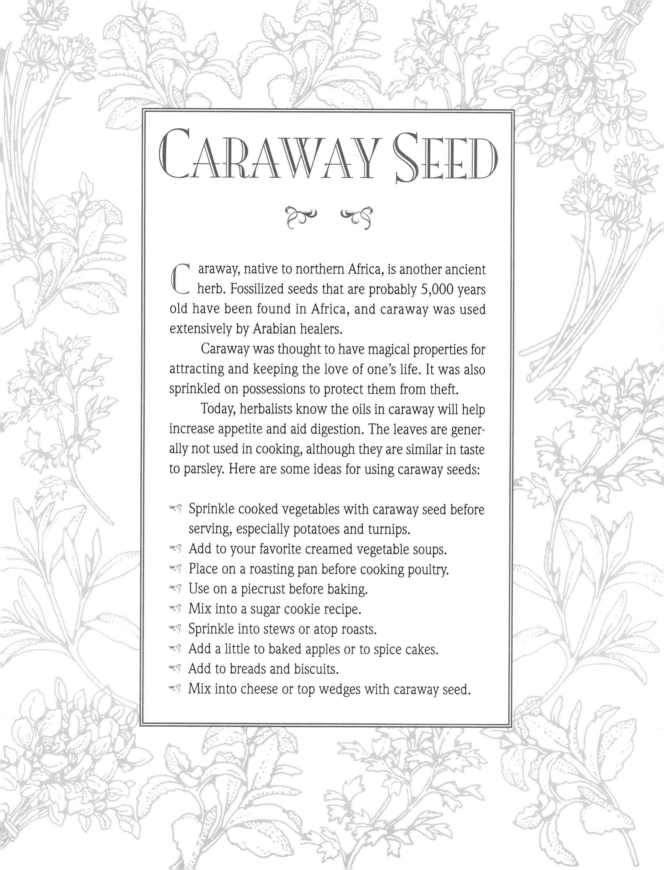

Caraway, native to northern Africa, is another ancient herb. Fossilized seeds that are probably 5,000 years old have been found in Africa, and caraway was used extensively by Arabian healers.

Caraway was thought to have magical properties for attracting and keeping the love of one's life. It was also sprinkled on possessions to protect them from theft.

Today, herbalists know the oils in caraway will help increase appetite and aid digestion. The leaves are generally not used in cooking, although they are similar in taste to parsley. Here are some ideas for using caraway seeds:

- Sprinkle cooked vegetables with caraway seed before serving, especially potatoes and turnips.
- Add to your favorite creamed vegetable soups.
- Place on a roasting pan before cooking poultry.
- Use on a piecrust before baking.
- Mix into a sugar cookie recipe.
- Sprinkle into stews or atop roasts.
- Add a little to baked apples or to spice cakes.
- Add to breads and biscuits.
- Mix into cheese or top wedges with caraway seed.

Cabbage and Caraway Slaw

2 cups cabbage, thinly sliced

1 cup jicama, peeled and thinly sliced

2½ tablespoons vegetable oil

2 teaspoons white wine vinegar

1 teaspoon fresh lemon juice

½ teaspoon caraway seeds

PREPARATION TIME:
Less than 30 minutes

Caraway seeds give this slaw a new taste. Serve on the side with any heavy foods or meats.

Toss cabbage and jicama together in a bowl. Whisk together remaining ingredients, then toss with the slaw.

Serves 4 to 6

66	Calories
0.5 g	Protein
3.3 g	Carbohydrates
6.0 g	Fat
81%	Calories from Fat
0.6 g	Fiber
5 mg	Sodium
0 mg	Cholesterol

Caraway Chicken and Noodles

❧ ❦

1 pound wide egg noodles
1½ cups shredded cooked
    chicken
3 tablespoons butter,
    melted
1 tablespoon caraway
    seeds
3 tablespoons chopped
    parsley
1 tablespoon freshly
    ground pepper

PREPARATION TIME:
Less than 30 minutes

I use skinless chicken breasts sautéed in a little butter and oil for this. It's a simple way to use leftover chicken as well.

Cook noodles according to package instructions and drain. Heat the cooked chicken. Add chicken to pasta, then toss with remaining ingredients.

Serves 4 to 6

398	Calories
20.6 g	Protein
54.2 g	Carbohydrates
10.8 g	Fat
24%	Calories from Fat
3.8 g	Fiber
100 mg	Sodium
114 mg	Cholesterol

CHERVIL

Chervil is a native of southern Europe and is used more in France than anywhere else in the world. Chervil is almost always an ingredient when the French prepare a *fines herbes*. Chervil blesses the gardener with tiny white flowers, but it is the leaves that provide a culinary use. This herb has a long medicinal history—Pliny believed the hiccoughs would be stopped by drinking vinegar with chervil. It was used in Europe as a remedy for upset stomachs, which may be true since chervil contains volatile oils, an aid to digestion.

The herb is easily grown and, while once scarce, it is appearing more frequently in supermarket produce sections. Chervil has a faint fragrance of anise. It should be added to dishes just before serving, never boiled. Things you can do with chervil include:

- Add to herb mixtures, including *fines herbes.*
- Mix into salads, including green, vegetable, and potato.
- Sprinkle on soups; stir into minestrone.
- Mix into omelets and scrambled eggs.
- Chervil goes well with fish, and in dressings for fish.
- Add chervil to vinaigrettes and other dressings.
- Use chervil as a replacement for parsley in some recipes.
- Chervil is good in many sauces, including cream sauces.

Chervil Cream Dressing

✌ ✌

4 tablespoons cream
2 tablespoons lemon juice
2 tablespoons plain yogurt
1 teaspoon honey
1½ tablespoons fresh
    minced chervil

PREPARATION TIME:
Less than 30 minutes

Add this dressing to vegetables or a green salad. If you don't have chervil, substitute parsley.

Combine all ingredients well.

Makes about ½ cup (2 tablespoons per serving)

Nutritional analysis is based on using half-and-half instead of cream.

30	Calories
0.9 g	Protein
3.2 g	Carbohydrates
1.7 g	Fat
50%	Calories from Fat
0.1 g	Fiber
12 mg	Sodium
5 mg	Cholesterol

Chickpea Salad with Chervil and Tarragon

2 cups cooked chickpeas,
   drained and rinsed
1 tablespoon minced chervil
½ teaspoon minced fresh
   tarragon
2 teaspoons minced fresh
   parsley
5 to 6 green onions, minced
¼ cup tarragon or white
   wine vinegar
1 teaspoon Dijon mustard
4 tablespoons extra-virgin
   olive oil

PREPARATION TIME:
Less than 30 minutes

This quick little salad goes well with Middle Eastern dishes, alongside meats, or as part of a vegetarian salad plate.

Combine chickpeas with herbs and green onions. Mix remaining ingredients, whisking well to combine. Toss dressing with chickpea mixture. Serve at room temperature.

Makes about 2 cups (4 servings)

261	Calories
7.5 g	Protein
24.1 g	Carbohydrates
15.8 g	Fat
55%	Calories from Fat
3.1 g	Fiber
40 mg	Sodium
0 mg	Cholesterol

Fruit with Chervil Dressing

$\approx$ $\ll$

¹⁄₄ cup white wine vinegar
2 tablespoons lemon juice
2 teaspoons honey
¹⁄₄ teaspoon ground nutmeg
¹⁄₂ teaspoon lemon zest
¹⁄₃ cup olive oil
  Pinch fresh marjoram
1 teaspoon fresh chopped
  chervil

PREPARATION TIME:
Less than 30 minutes

Slice up pears, peaches, bananas, grapes, melons, or whatever you have on hand and top with this dressing.

Combine vinegar, lemon juice, honey, nutmeg, and zest and mix well. Slowly add oil and whisk to blend. Stir in herbs and pour over fruit.

Makes about ¹⁄₂ cup (2 tablespoons per serving)

174	Calories
0.1 g	Protein
4.6 g	Carbohydrates
18.0 g	Fat
93%	Calories from Fat
0.0 g	Fiber
0 mg	Sodium
0 mg	Cholesterol

Carrots and Zucchini with Herb Dressing

3 small zucchini, thinly
    sliced
4 to 5 carrots, thinly sliced
½ sweet onion, thinly sliced
1 shallot, minced
3 tablespoons extra-virgin
    olive oil
4 teaspoons minced celery
½ teaspoon *each* minced
    parsley, chervil,
    marjoram, and sage
2 tablespoons wine vinegar
    Salt and pepper

PREPARATION TIME:
Less than 30 minutes

Fresh herbs are recommended for this vegetable sauce. If you must substitute some dried, used a little less than half the suggested amount.

Toss the zucchini, carrots, and onion in a bowl. Sauté the shallot in 1 tablespoon of oil for 3 to 4 minutes, then add the celery and herbs. Stir well, add vinegar, mix, and remove from heat. Whisk in remaining oil, salt, and pepper, and pour over vegetables.

Serves 4

140	Calories
1.7	g Protein
12.0	g Carbohydrates
10.4	g Fat
66%	Calories from Fat
3.4	g Fiber
30	mg Sodium
0	mg Cholesterol

Chervil

Chicken Soup with Lemon and Chervil

7 cups chicken stock
1 onion, peeled
2 stalks celery, halved
1 carrot, chopped
1 bay leaf
1 pound boneless, skinless
    chicken breasts, sliced
  Zest from 1 lemon
2 tablespoons lemon juice
3 tablespoons sliced chives
    or green onions
2 tablespoons minced chervil

PREPARATION TIME:
Less than 1 hour

I like to use citrus for flavoring dishes, especially lemon and lime, which go well with so many things. Here's a chicken soup I created that has a little lemon flavor.

Bring stock to a boil and add the onion, celery, carrot, and bay leaf. Cover and simmer 25 minutes. Add chicken and simmer for another 12 minutes, until just cooked. Remove onion, celery, and bay leaf, and add zest, lemon juice, and chives. Cook another 1 to 2 minutes, then transfer to a bowl and sprinkle with chervil.

Serves 4

182	Calories
30.6 g	Protein
10.6 g	Carbohydrates
1.6 g	Fat
8%	Calories from Fat
1.7 g	Fiber
238 mg	Sodium
65 mg	Cholesterol

Cooking with Herbs

CHIVES

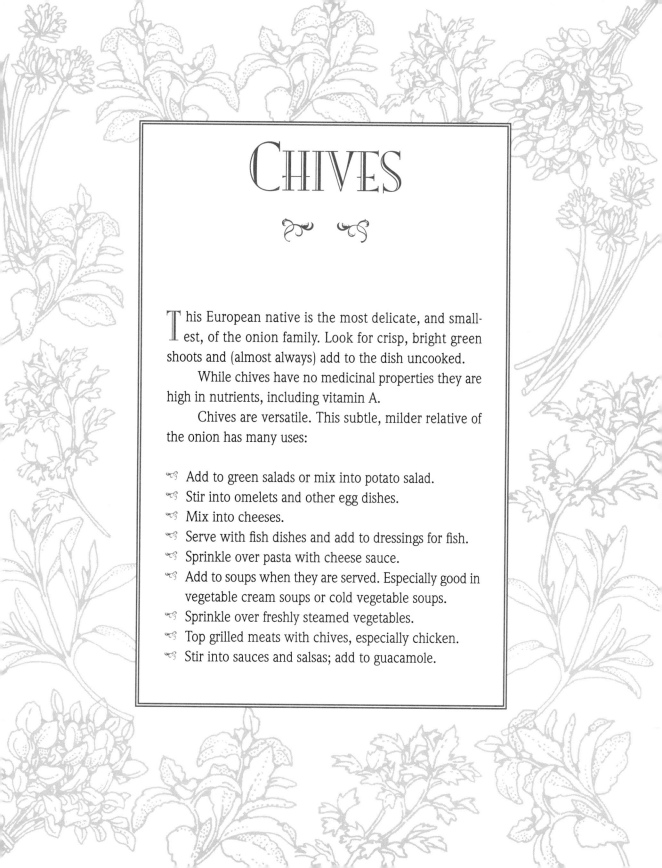

This European native is the most delicate, and small-est, of the onion family. Look for crisp, bright green shoots and (almost always) add to the dish uncooked.

While chives have no medicinal properties they are high in nutrients, including vitamin A.

Chives are versatile. This subtle, milder relative of the onion has many uses:

- Add to green salads or mix into potato salad.
- Stir into omelets and other egg dishes.
- Mix into cheeses.
- Serve with fish dishes and add to dressings for fish.
- Sprinkle over pasta with cheese sauce.
- Add to soups when they are served. Especially good in vegetable cream soups or cold vegetable soups.
- Sprinkle over freshly steamed vegetables.
- Top grilled meats with chives, especially chicken.
- Stir into sauces and salsas; add to guacamole.

Black Bean Dip

৵ ৵

3 cups cooked black beans

⅓ cup plain yogurt or sour cream

3 tablespoons chives, chopped

¼ teaspoon fresh marjoram, or ⅛ teaspoon dried

¼ teaspoon fresh thyme, or ⅛ teaspoon dried

⅛ teaspoon salt

PREPARATION TIME:
Less than 30 minutes

Black beans are a cook's best friend. They can be used in an emergency to make a variety of great things—I always have some on hand. Serve vegetables with this dip.

Combine all ingredients in a food processor or blender and purée. Add a little more yogurt if it is too thick.

Makes about 3 cups (2 tablespoons per serving)

30	Calories
2.1 g	Protein
5.3 g	Carbohydrates
0.1 g	Fat
4%	Calories from Fat
0.9 g	Fiber
13 mg	Sodium
0 mg	Cholesterol

Jicama and Melon Salsa

2 cups peeled and diced jicama

1½ cups diced honeydew or watermelon

2 tablespoons minced chives

1 tablespoon minced cilantro

2 tablespoons fresh lime juice

PREPARATION TIME:
Less than 30 minutes

This is a refreshing switch from spicy salsas. Serve it with spicy foods.

Combine all ingredients.

Makes about 4 cups (2 tablespoons per serving)

5	Calories
0.1 g	Protein
1.3 g	Carbohydrates
0.0 g	Fat
3%	Calories from Fat
0.1 g	Fiber
1 mg	Sodium
0 mg	Cholesterol

Red Pepper Soup

୧୬ ୭୯

1 medium onion, diced
1 small carrot, diced
1 stalk celery, diced
1/8 cup olive oil
4 red peppers, seeded and
 chopped
1/4 teaspoon Tabasco or other
 hot pepper sauce,
 to taste
1 pound red potatoes,
 peeled and cut into
 1/8-inch slices
2 cups vegetable broth
3 cups water
1/2 teaspoon thyme
1/4 teaspoon pepper
1/2 lemon, thinly sliced
3 tablespoons chopped
 chives

PREPARATION TIME:
Less than 30 minutes

My dear friend Amy Driscoll likes to add a lemon slice, which goes perfectly with this colorful soup.

Sauté the onion, carrot, and celery in olive oil until soft, about 8 minutes. Add remaining ingredients and bring to a boil. Reduce heat and simmer about 30 minutes, or until all the vegetables are soft. Place in a blender or food processor in batches and purée. Reheat and serve with a slice of lemon and a sprinkling of chives in each bowl.

Serves 4 to 6

134	Calories
2.8 g	Protein
21.6 g	Carbohydrates
4.8 g	Fat
32%	Calories from Fat
3.0 g	Fiber
21 mg	Sodium
0 mg	Cholesterol

Green Beans and Chives

❧ ❧

1 pound green beans, trimmed
3 tablespoons butter
¼ cup diced celery
½ teaspoon fresh thyme, or a pinch dried
2 tablespoons minced parsley
2 tablespoons minced chives

PREPARATION TIME:
Less than 30 minutes

I seem to prepare green bean dishes around holiday dinners. This is one I've made for Thanksgiving.

Cook beans in boiling water until crisp-tender, about 10 minutes. Melt butter in a skillet and add celery. Sauté 2 minutes, then add remaining ingredients. Sauté 4 to 5 minutes. Toss with beans.

Serves 4 to 6

83	Calories
1.6 g	Protein
6.3 g	Carbohydrates
6.3 g	Fat
69%	Calories from Fat
1.5 g	Fiber
69 mg	Sodium
17 mg	Cholesterol

Curried Zucchini Soup

3 cups chicken stock
4 zucchini, cut into thick slices
1 onion, chopped
1½ tablespoons curry powder (see Basic Recipes)
6 mushrooms, sliced
1 tablespoon butter or oil
¾ cup milk or cream
1 tablespoon pepper
⅓ cup chopped chives

PREPARATION TIME:
Less than 1 hour

I enjoy curry flavors in many dishes, and in this soup it works well. Pre-cook chunks of chicken and add to the soup, if desired.

Place stock in a saucepan and add zucchini, onion, and spices. Bring to a boil, cover, and simmer 20 minutes, stirring occasionally. Meanwhile, sauté mushrooms in butter or oil until color changes, about 5 minutes. Place the zucchini mixture into a blender and purée. Strain if desired, then stir in the milk, mushrooms, and pepper. Sprinkle with chives.

Serves 4 to 6

72	Calories
3.8 g	Protein
8.7 g	Carbohydrates
3.1 g	Fat
39%	Calories from Fat
1.5 g	Fiber
84 mg	Sodium
8 mg	Cholesterol

Spinach Risotto

☙ ❧

1½ cups fresh or frozen
    chopped spinach
5 cups vegetable or
    chicken stock
1 tablespoon olive oil
1½ cups arborio or other
    short grain rice
1 leek, chopped
⅛ teaspoon ground
    coriander
⅛ teaspoon ground mace
¼ teaspoon grated ginger
½ cup minced chives
    Parmesan cheese
    (optional)

PREPARATION TIME:
Less than 1 hour

I like to serve this with Parmesan, and as a side dish to a simply prepared meat.

Blanch the spinach if fresh; cook if frozen. Set aside. Bring the stock to a boil, remove from heat. Heat oil in a frying pan and add rice, leek, and spices. Sauté until the rice is golden, about 4 minutes. Add enough stock to cover the rice. Simmer gently and stir constantly, until the liquid is absorbed. Repeat process, adding a cup of stock at a time, until all of the stock is used. Stir in the cooked spinach and chives. Top with Parmesan cheese if desired.

Serves 4 to 6

204	Calories
4.1 g	Protein
39.9 g	Carbohydrates
2.7 g	Fat
12%	Calories from Fat
1.2 g	Fiber
16 mg	Sodium
0 mg	Cholesterol

Cinnamon

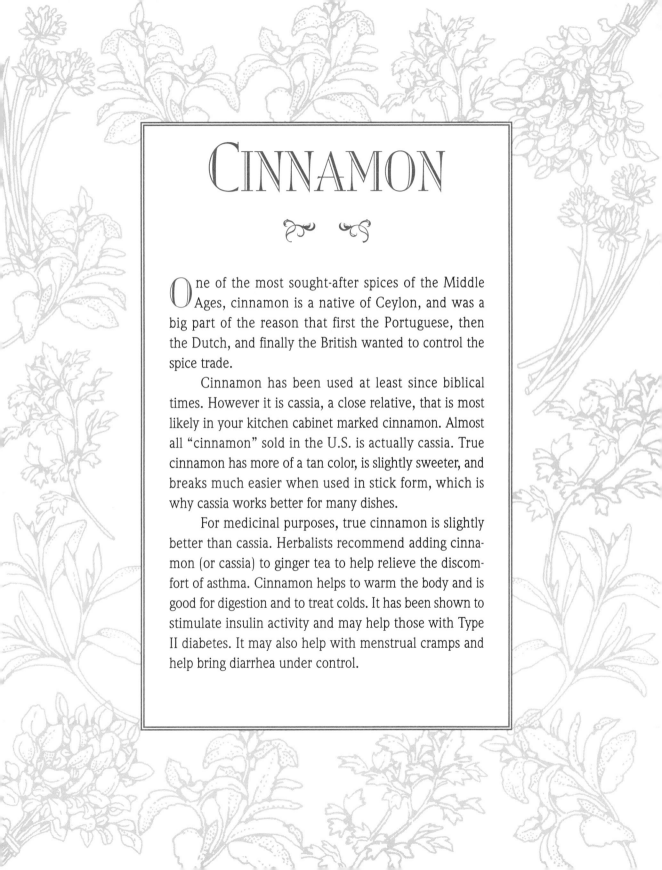

One of the most sought-after spices of the Middle Ages, cinnamon is a native of Ceylon, and was a big part of the reason that first the Portuguese, then the Dutch, and finally the British wanted to control the spice trade.

Cinnamon has been used at least since biblical times. However it is cassia, a close relative, that is most likely in your kitchen cabinet marked cinnamon. Almost all "cinnamon" sold in the U.S. is actually cassia. True cinnamon has more of a tan color, is slightly sweeter, and breaks much easier when used in stick form, which is why cassia works better for many dishes.

For medicinal purposes, true cinnamon is slightly better than cassia. Herbalists recommend adding cinnamon (or cassia) to ginger tea to help relieve the discomfort of asthma. Cinnamon helps to warm the body and is good for digestion and to treat colds. It has been shown to stimulate insulin activity and may help those with Type II diabetes. It may also help with menstrual cramps and help bring diarrhea under control.

Here are some ways to add cinnamon to your diet:

- Use a cinnamon stick as a swizzle stick for cider, cocoa, coffee, or hot chocolate.
- Add some to your milkshake.
- Use in desserts, including pies and puddings.
- Sprinkle over fruits such as baked apples or pineapple.
- Stir into cranberry sauce.
- Cook sticks with meats, especially pork.
- Add to meat stews.
- Stir a little into soups, especially broths.
- Sprinkle on vegetables before baking.
- Add to dessert sauces.

Cold Blueberry–Cinnamon Soup

꙰ ꙰

1 pint blueberries
1½ cups water
2 tablespoons sugar
3 tablespoons honey
⅛ teaspoon ground cloves
⅛ teaspoon allspice
½ teaspoon cinnamon
2 tablespoons lime juice
1 tablespoon cornstarch
    dissolved in 3 table-
    spoons warm water

PREPARATION TIME:
Less than 30 minutes

This unusual combination makes a stunning starter before a barbecue or other summer meal.

Combine all ingredients in a pot, except lime juice and cornstarch, and bring to a boil. Reduce heat, crush blueberries with the back of a wooden spoon, cover, and simmer 15 minutes, stirring occasionally. Add lime juice and cornstarch, return to a boil, then remove from heat. Chill before serving.

Serves 4

123 Calories
0.6 g Protein
31.8 g Carbohydrates
0.3 g Fat
2% Calories from Fat
1.8 g Fiber
8 mg Sodium
0 mg Cholesterol

Valerie's Pumpkin Bread

3½ cups flour
2¼ cups sugar
1 heaping teaspoon
   baking soda
1½ tablespoons cinnamon
¼ teaspoon allspice
½ teaspoon ground cloves
1⅛ cups raisins
1⅛ cups chopped dates
1⅛ cups chopped walnuts
4 large eggs
1 (15-ounce) can pumpkin
⅔ cup water
⅔ cup oil

PREPARATION TIME:
Less than 30 minutes
(plus baking time)

My friend Valerie Wicklund had this bread recipe passed on to her from her grandmother. The recipe has always been made in coffee cans, but it can be made in a bread pan as well.

Preheat oven to 350 degrees. Grease and flour three (1 pound) coffee cans, or bread pans. Combine the flour, sugar, soda, cinnamon, allspice, and cloves in a large bowl until mixed well. Add raisins, dates, and walnuts until they are well coated with the flour mixture. Make a large hole in the middle and add the eggs, pumpkin, water, and oil. Mix well with a spoon, fill each can or pan about two thirds full, and bake 1 hour and 15 minutes, or until a toothpick inserted into each loaf comes out clean.

Makes 3 loaves (48 slices)

144 Calories
1.8 g Protein
21.4 g Carbohydrates
6.2 g Fat
39% Calories from Fat
0.9 g Fiber
40 mg Sodium
17 mg Cholesterol

Cooking with Herbs

Cinnamon Rice

୧୨ ୧୨

1 tablespoon butter
⅓ cup diced carrots
½ cup diced sweet or
    Spanish onion
1½ cups long-grain rice
2 sticks cinnamon
⅓ cup raisins
4½ cups water

PREPARATION TIME:
Less than 1 hour

The rice absorbs the cinnamon flavor nicely in this dish, which I serve with pork.

Melt the butter and sauté the carrots and onion over medium-low heat until soft, about 8 minutes. Add remaining ingredients and bring to a boil. Allow mixture to simmer 10 minutes, uncovered; then cover, reduce heat to low, and cook 15 minutes, stirring occasionally, until rice is done. Remove cinnamon sticks and serve.

Serves 4

332	Calories
5.8 g	Protein
68.4 g	Carbohydrates
3.6 g	Fat
10%	Calories from Fat
1.8 g	Fiber
51 mg	Sodium
8 mg	Cholesterol

Judy's Creamy Sweet Potato Soup

≈ ≈

2 tablespoons butter or oil

3 tablespoons minced onion

1 small celery stalk, minced

1¾ cups water

1½ cups chicken broth

3 cups sweet potatoes, peeled and thinly sliced

½ cup hot milk

1 tablespoon molasses

2 teaspoons freshly grated ginger

½ teaspoon *each* allspice and cinnamon

2 tablespoons orange juice

PREPARATION TIME:
Less than 1 hour

A librarian friend inspired this recipe for a soup using sweet potatoes.

Heat the butter or oil in a saucepan. Sauté the onion and celery until soft, about 5 minutes. Add the water, broth, and potatoes and bring to a boil. Reduce heat and simmer for 20 minutes, or until sweet potatoes are very tender. Remove from heat and stir in remaining ingredients. Purée in batches, then return to saucepan and warm.

Serves 4

206	Calories
3.9 g	Protein
32.4 g	Carbohydrates
7.1 g	Fat
31%	Calories from Fat
3.4 g	Fiber
142 mg	Sodium
19 mg	Cholesterol

Cooking with Herbs

Cranberry Sauce

⟡

⅓ cup sugar
⅓ cup brown sugar
½ teaspoon cinnamon
2 tablespoons lime juice
2 tablespoons lemon juice
¾ cup water
3 cups fresh
    cranberries—
      one (12-ounce) bag
2 teaspoons vanilla

PREPARATION TIME:
Less than 30 minutes

I seldom buy cranberry sauce, since making it is so simple. Prepare this and put some in your child's school lunch the next day.

Bring the sugars, juices, cinnamon, and water to a boil. Add cranberries and simmer uncovered, stirring occasionally, until cranberries are tender, about 8 minutes. Remove from heat and stir in vanilla.

Makes about 2½ cups (¼ cup per serving)

71	Calories
0.1 g	Protein
18.1 g	Carbohydrates
0.1 g	Fat
1%	Calories from Fat
1.4 g	Fiber
4 mg	Sodium
0 mg	Cholesterol

Orange Carrots and Red Peppers

1 large sweet red pepper
6 to 7 carrots, peeled and
    thinly sliced
  Juice of $\frac{1}{2}$ orange
$\frac{1}{4}$ teaspoon cinnamon
2 teaspoons honey
3 tablespoons butter
$\frac{1}{4}$ teaspoon pepper
  Zest of $\frac{1}{2}$ orange

PREPARATION TIME:
Less than 1 hour

This unusual combination goes well as a side dish to many entrées, or use it on a vegetarian plate.

Using a vegetable peeler, remove the skin from the pepper. Seed and slice. Place carrots in a saucepan with the orange juice, cinnamon, honey, butter, and pepper. Add $\frac{2}{3}$ cup water and bring to a boil. Cover and cook 10 minutes, or until carrots are tender. Remove lid and cook until liquid is gone. Stir in the red pepper and zest. Mix well and serve.

Serves 4 to 6

108	Calories
1.2 g	Protein
12.9 g	Carbohydrates
6.3 g	Fat
52%	Calories from Fat
1.4 g	Fiber
114 mg	Sodium
17 mg	Cholesterol

Cinnamon–Apple Sweet Potatoes

❧ ❧

4 sweet potatoes
1½ cups finely chopped
Granny Smith or
other cooking apples
¼ cup lemon juice
¼ cup orange juice
Zest of 1 lemon
2 tablespoons honey
½ teaspoon cinnamon

PREPARATION TIME:
Less than 30 minutes
(plus baking time)

Cinnamon, apples, and sweet potatoes are another natural marriage. I came up with this combination one winter and have repeated it several times.

Clean and prick the potatoes, and bake at 375 degrees for 1 hour, or until done. Meanwhile, combine remaining ingredients and mix well. Microwave for 4 minutes, stirring once. Pour the apple mixture over the split potatoes.

Serves 4

218	Calories
2.6 g	Protein
53.0 g	Carbohydrates
0.6 g	Fat
3%	Calories from Fat
5.3 g	Fiber
19 mg	Sodium
0 mg	Cholesterol

Cinnamon Muffins with Hazelnuts

❧ ❧

3 cups flour
1½ cups brown sugar
⅛ teaspoon ground allspice
½ teaspoon ground ginger
2½ teaspoons ground cinnamon
⅔ cup shortening
½ cup chopped toasted hazelnuts
2 teaspoons baking powder
½ teaspoon baking soda
2 eggs, beaten
1 cup buttermilk

PREPARATION TIME:
Less than 30 minutes
(plus baking time)

Cinnamon has a warming effect on the body and these muffins are a blessing for sniffles in the family on a Sunday morning.

Preheat oven to 375 degrees. Oil muffin tins. Combine flour, sugar, allspice, ginger, and 1½ teaspoons of the cinnamon. Add shortening and mix well. Remove ¾ cup to a separate bowl. Mix in the nuts and remaining cinnamon and set aside for use as a topping. To the remaining mixture, add baking powder and baking soda. Add eggs and buttermilk. Spoon into the muffin tins. Sprinkle each muffin with a little of the reserved topping and bake for 15 minutes, or until a toothpick inserted into the center comes out clean.

Makes about 18 muffins

255 Calories
3.7 g Protein
36.6 g Carbohydrates
10.7 g Fat
38% Calories from Fat
0.9 g Fiber
101 mg Sodium
24 mg Cholesterol

Cooking with Herbs

Tomato Sauce with Cinnamon

¼ cup extra-virgin olive oil
1 small onion
6 to 8 tomatoes
2 cloves garlic, crushed
1 tablespoon sugar
¼ cup red wine
2 cinnamon sticks
2 tablespoons fresh oregano
3 tablespoons fresh
   chopped basil

PREPARATION TIME:
Less than 30 minutes
(plus simmer time)

I came up with this after learning that many Greek cooks like to add cinnamon to their tomato sauces. There is a good reason for it; cinnamon goes surprisingly well with tomato sauces.

Sauté the onion in oil until soft, then add tomatoes, garlic, sugar, red wine, cinnamon sticks, and oregano. Add ½ cup water and bring to a boil, then simmer gently for 1 hour, stirring occasionally, adding more water if needed. Stir in fresh basil and cook another 10 minutes, then remove the cinnamon and garlic. Serve over pasta.

Serves 4 to 6

125	Calories
1.4 g	Protein
10.0 g	Carbohydrates
9.5 g	Fat
68%	Calories from Fat
2.0 g	Fiber
12 mg	Sodium
0 mg	Cholesterol

Cinnamon Apple Chutney

❧ ❧

3 cups diced apples
1 cup cider vinegar
1 teaspoon cinnamon
¼ teaspoon cloves
½ cup raisins
½ cup brown sugar
¼ cup minced fresh ginger
Juice of 1 lemon

PREPARATION TIME:
Less than 1 hour

Use a tart apple when making this chutney since sweeter types don't match the flavors as well. This is nice with pork dishes, or as an appetizer.

Put all ingredients in a saucepan on low-medium heat and simmer about 45 minutes, or until apples are soft.

Makes about 3 cups (1 tablespoon per serving)

21	Calories
0.1 g	Protein
5.4 g	Carbohydrates
0.0 g	Fat
0%	Calories from Fat
0.3 g	Fiber
1 mg	Sodium
0 mg	Cholesterol

Lemon Cinnamon Pears

Juice of 1 lemon
1 lemon, sliced
8 pears, peeled and cored
¾ cup sugar
2 cinnamon sticks
6 cups water

PREPARATION TIME:
Less than 1 hour
(plus chilling time)

This is a warm and always well received dessert. My boys like almost anything with cinnamon in it.

Place all ingredients in a pot, and bring to a boil. Reduce heat to low, cover, and simmer 30 minutes. Remove pears, then return lemon mixture to boiling. Cook until reduced to 3 cups, about 20 minutes. Discard solids and pour syrup over the pears. Chill for at least 3 hours. Serve chilled.

Serves 8

168 Calories
0.7 g Protein
43.6 g Carbohydrates
0.7 g Fat
3% Calories from Fat
4.3 g Fiber
4 mg Sodium
0 mg Cholesterol

CORIANDER/ CILANTRO

Coriander is one of the world's oldest recorded spices. Seeds from the spice have been found in Egyptian tombs dating back to 1000 B.C. The Bible mentions coriander and some food historians believe it may in fact be the oldest spice, with references to 4000 B.C.

This Mediterranean native was used to preserve meat in the Middle Ages (despite the fact that the superstitious thought coriander would make a person avaricious).

In the United States *coriander* usually refers to the seed of the plant, dried and ground. *Cilantro* is the fresh leaf. The herb is also known as Chinese parsley in Asia, fresh coriander in India, and simply as coriander through most of Europe.

Coriander is helpful to digestion and reduces flatulence. It also stimulates the appetite by aiding the secretion of gastric juices.

Coriander is found in many foods and may be added to others:

- ❧ When making a curry powder make sure to include ground coriander.
- ❧ Add a little of the ground spice to biscuits, scones, or any sweet bread.
- ❧ Stir ground coriander into tapioca, or sprinkle on top.
- ❧ Add fresh or ground to any Mexican sauce. Use with any fresh Mexican food, sprinkling on chopped cilantro last.
- ❧ Add fresh chopped cilantro to salads, or sprinkle over fruit.
- ❧ Stir some ground coriander into applesauce.
- ❧ Add ground coriander to cookie and gingerbread recipes.
- ❧ Ground coriander is good in many sauces and relishes, including fruit sauces. Add fresh cilantro to salsas and guacamole.
- ❧ Sprinkle ground coriander onto pea soup, or stir into other soups, especially lentil and bean.

Lime–Cilantro Pasta Salad

❧ ☙

½ pound farfalle (bowtie) pasta
¼ cup plus 1 tablespoon extra-virgin olive oil
3 small tomatoes, chopped
⅓ cup fresh chopped cilantro
3 green onions, chopped
¼ teaspoon hot pepper sauce
2 tablespoons lime juice
1 tablespoon lime zest

PREPARATION TIME:
Less than 1 hour

This delicious dish is especially great and colorful with Mexican dishes or grilled foods.

Cook pasta according to package directions; drain, rinse, and toss with the 1 tablespoon of olive oil and cool to room temperature. Combine tomatoes, cilantro, and green onions and mix well by hand or in a food processor. Combine the remaining olive oil, hot pepper sauce, lime juice, and zest, and toss with pasta. Serve at room temperature or slightly chilled.

Serves 4

369	Calories
7.6 g	Protein
45.3 g	Carbohydrates
18.1 g	Fat
44%	Calories from Fat
5.2 g	Fiber
15 mg	Sodium
0 mg	Cholesterol

Breakfast Burritos

1 teaspoon vegetable oil
5 green onions, chopped
2 red potatoes, cooked
    and diced
1 tomato, diced
2 mild chiles, peeled,
    seeded, and chopped
    (canned okay)
4 eggs, lightly beaten
1/4 teaspoon ground cumin
2 tablespoons fresh
    chopped cilantro
4 flour tortillas
    Fresh salsa (optional)
    Sour cream (optional)
    Cheddar cheese (optional)

PREPARATION TIME:
Less than 1 hour

I don't make these often enough, but when I do they are a hit. Potatoes mixed into burritos and tortillas are popular in Mexico and here you can see why.

Heat oil in a skillet and add green onions, potatoes, tomatoes, and chiles. Sauté until warm, 3 to 4 minutes. Push vegetables to the sides and add eggs to the skillet. Sprinkle with cumin, then cook, stirring, until done as desired. Stir cooked eggs and vegetables together; sprinkle with cilantro. Mix and serve topped with salsa, sour cream, or grated cheese if you like.

Makes 4 burritos

355	Calories
14.2 g	Protein
47.5 g	Carbohydrates
11.0 g	Fat
27%	Calories from Fat
6.9 g	Fiber
257 mg	Sodium
213 mg	Cholesterol

Cooking with Herbs

Crab Gazpacho with Cilantro

❦ ❦

2 sweet onions
1 cucumber, peeled and
   seeded
2 sweet peppers, seeded
5 small ripe tomatoes,
   peeled
3 cloves garlic, minced or
   chopped
2 jalapeños, seeded and
   coarsely chopped
2 cups tomato juice
$\frac{1}{3}$ cup extra-virgin olive oil
$\frac{1}{4}$ teaspoon salt
$\frac{1}{4}$ teaspoon pepper
$\frac{1}{2}$ pound cooked crabmeat
$\frac{1}{4}$ cup fresh chopped
   cilantro

PREPARATION TIME:
Less than 1 hour
(plus chilling time)

For great gazpacho, don't overprocess the vegetables; make sure they retain some texture and crunch. Chopping by hand is best for this. Crab makes a nice addition to this gazpacho, but vegetarians can leave it out.

Finely chop the onions, cucumber, sweet peppers, and three of the tomatoes and place in a bowl. In a blender or food processor, add the remaining ingredients and purée, then combine the chopped vegetables with the purée. Fold the crabmeat into the soup. Sprinkle a little cilantro onto each serving.

Serves 6

223	Calories
10.7 g	Protein
18.0 g	Carbohydrates
13.3 g	Fat
53%	Calories from Fat
3.7 g	Fiber
499 mg	Sodium
38 mg	Cholesterol

Black Bean Tostadas with Spicy Corn Salsa

⁊⟶ ⟵⟅

12 corn tortillas
   Vegetable oil
2 cups (about 4 ears) fresh
   corn, cooked, or
   1 (10-ounce) package
   of kernels, defrosted
1 jalapeño or other hot
   pepper, seeded and
   minced
½ teaspoon salt
½ teaspoon pepper
3 roma tomatoes, thinly
   sliced with the slices
   halved
⅓ cup chopped sweet or
   red onion
⅓ cup chopped sweet
   pepper, green, yellow,
   or red
3 tablespoons minced
   cilantro
2 tablespoons fresh lime
   juice
2 teaspoons lime zest
2 tablespoons extra-virgin
   olive oil
2 cups black beans or
   refried beans
2 cups grated cheddar or
   jack cheese (optional)

PREPARATION TIME:
Less than 1 hour

I love to make tostadas and like to put on them anything I happen to have handy—from peaches to daikon. This is a tried-and-true recipe for great Mexican food.

Heat enough oil over medium heat in a skillet to cover the pan. Cook tortillas in the hot oil one at a time until crisp, about 1 minute each, on each side. Dry on paper towels and reserve.

Combine the remaining ingredients (except the beans and cheese) and mix well. Let sit at least 30 minutes. Heat the black beans and spread on the cooked tortillas, adding a sprinkling of cheese if desired. Spread with corn salsa and serve.

Makes 12 tostadas

158	Calories
4.9 g	Protein
25.8 g	Carbohydrates
4.3 g	Fat
24%	Calories from Fat
3.6 g	Fiber
146 mg	Sodium
0 mg	Cholesterol

Chile Chicken Toss

3 poblano chiles
2 tablespoons olive oil
2 tablespoons good-quality
   chile powder
1 teaspoon cumin
2 cloves garlic, minced
⅓ cup lime juice
2 boneless, skinless chicken
   breasts, cut into strips
¼ cup cilantro, chopped
   Corn tortillas

PREPARATION TIME:
Less than 30 minutes

This is a quick dinner and the blackened chiles taste great tossed with the chicken and spices. Serve in or with tortillas, and with rice and beans, or a salad if desired.

Slit the chiles on one side and discard the seed pod. Place under a broiler and blacken on each side, or barbecue on a lightly oiled grill. Cut the chiles into strips and keep warm.

Add the oil, chile powder, cumin, garlic, and lime juice to a skillet and mix well. Sauté the chicken until done. Remove from heat and toss with chile strips and cilantro. Serve in or along-side tortillas.

Serves 4

Nutritional analysis does not include tortillas.

211	Calories
28.2 g	Protein
5.8 g	Carbohydrates
8.4 g	Fat
35%	Calories from Fat
0.7 g	Fiber
80 mg	Sodium
68 mg	Cholesterol

Chicken with Tomatillo White Sauce

૨૭ ૯૪

1 pound (about 11) fresh
   tomatillos, husked and
   washed
1 jalapeño, seeded
1 mild Anaheim chile,
   seeded and halved
5 sprigs fresh cilantro
1/2 teaspoon allspice
1 small onion, chopped
1 clove garlic, chopped or
   minced
1 tablespoon vegetable oil
2 cups broth
2 boneless, skinless chicken
   breasts, halved
1/2 cup sour cream

PREPARATION TIME:
Less than 1 hour

Tomatillos are underused by Americans. These little green tomatoes simply need to be husked to be enjoyed in salsas, or softened in boiling water for use in sauces.

Cook the chicken breasts in a skillet or on the grill and keep warm. Boil the tomatillos and chiles in salted water until just tender, about 10 minutes. (If using canned tomatillos or chiles, simply drain.) Drain the tomatillos and place in a blender or processor with the cilantro, allspice, onion, and garlic and blend until smooth. Heat oil in a skillet over medium-high heat. Pour all of the sauce in and stir for 5 minutes. Add the broth, return to a boil, and reduce the heat to medium. Simmer until thick, about 10 minutes. Meanwhile, sauté or grill the chicken breasts until done. Place on a plate. Stir the sour cream into the tomatillo sauce. Pour over the chicken and serve.

Serves 4

246	Calories
29.9 g	Protein
13.3 g	Carbohydrates
8.2 g	Fat
30%	Calories from Fat
2.5 g	Fiber
112 mg	Sodium
74 mg	Cholesterol

Cooking with Herbs

Chile-Cheese Quesadillas with Avocado-Tomatillo Sauce

7 to 8 tomatillos, husked and washed
2 to 3 avocados, skinned, chopped, and pitted
¼ cup olive oil
Juice of ½ lemon
⅛ teaspoon cumin
2 cloves garlic, minced
½ cup chopped onion
½ cup chopped cilantro
8 flour tortillas
1 cup grated cheddar cheese
2 mild Anaheim chiles, peeled and sliced (canned okay)

PREPARATION TIME:
Less than 30 minutes

Use mild chiles for this sauce, since hot ones will overpower the mild taste of the avocado.

Cook the tomatillos in boiling water until soft, 7 to 8 minutes. Place all ingredients (except tortillas, cheese, and chiles) in a food processor or blender and purée.

To make the quesadillas, spread the cheese and chiles among four of the tortillas and spread evenly. Top each with a second tortilla. Heat a dry skillet and warm quesadillas on both sides, one at a time, until cheese melts. Serve with sauce on the side or poured over quesadillas. Serve immediately or chilled.

Makes 4 quesadillas and 3 cups of sauce

618	Calories
15.4 g	Protein
51.7 g	Carbohydrates
41.8 g	Fat
60%	Calories from Fat
5.6 g	Fiber
302 mg	Sodium
27 mg	Cholesterol

Grilled Swordfish with Pineapple–Cilantro Sauce

❧ ☙

2 pounds swordfish steaks
2 cups pineapple rings
2 tablespoons brown sugar
¼ teaspoon hot pepper
  sauce
½ cup water
1 tablespoon minced
  cilantro
1 teaspoon lime zest

PREPARATION TIME:
Less than 30 minutes

You can use this sauce on any mild-tasting fish. Broiling the pineapple gives it a rich tangy flavor.

Grill, broil, or pan-fry the swordfish. Place the pineapple on a lightly oiled baking sheet and broil for 5 minutes on each side, until brown. In a saucepan, bring the pineapple, brown sugar, pepper sauce, and water to a boil and simmer, stirring occasionally, 20 minutes. Cool, then purée. Stir in cilantro and zest. Serve alongside or poured over fish.

Serves 4

369	Calories
41.1 g	Protein
31.5 g	Carbohydrates
8.3 g	Fat
20%	Calories from Fat
0.3 g	Fiber
192 mg	Sodium
80 mg	Cholesterol

Cooking with Herbs

Black Bean Soup

❦ ❧

1 small onion, chopped
½ sweet red or yellow
    pepper, chopped
1 tablespoon oil
3 cups black beans (dried
    beans soaked overnight
    or canned beans rinsed
    and drained)
2 cloves garlic, minced
¼ cup tomato sauce
½ teaspoon mace
1 teaspoon allspice
    Juice of 1 lime
½ cup chopped cilantro

PREPARATION TIME:
Less than 30 minutes
(plus cooking time)

This simple soup is a snap to make. Serve with tortillas.

Sauté the onion and pepper in the oil just 3 to 4 minutes. Add all of the remaining ingredients, except lime and cilantro, and water to cover. Bring to a boil and simmer 1 hour, adding water if necessary for desired consistency. Stir in lime juice. Remove from heat and ladle into bowls. Sprinkle with cilantro.

Serves 4 to 6

153	Calories
8.2 g	Protein
24.9 g	Carbohydrates
3.0 g	Fat
17%	Calories from Fat
4.3 g	Fiber
64 mg	Sodium
0 mg	Cholesterol

Coriander/Cilantro

Chickpea and Cilantro Soup

꿍 꿍

2 tablespoons water
1 tablespoon cornstarch
2 tablespoons vegetable oil
1 (15-ounce) can chickpeas,
    drained
⅓ cup onion, chopped
1 teaspoon minced fresh
    ginger
1 teaspoon ground turmeric
½ teaspoon cinnamon
½ teaspoon nutmeg
¼ cup chopped parsley
6 cups chicken stock
½ cup rice
¾ cup crushed tomatoes
¼ cup fresh chopped
    cilantro

PREPARATION TIME:
Less than 1 hour
(plus simmering time)

The chickpeas, rice, and spices make this a warming soup.

Combine cornstarch and water and set aside. In a large pot add the oil, chickpeas, onion, spices, and parsley. Add water to cover, bring to a boil, cover, and simmer at least 1 hour.

In a separate pot, heat the stock to boiling and add the rice. Boil 15 minutes. Place the tomatoes and cilantro in food processor and purée. Add to the rice along with the cornstarch mixture. Cook another 10 minutes, stirring constantly. Add the rice combination to the pot and serve.

Serves 6

215	Calories
7.2 g	Protein
33.9 g	Carbohydrates
5.7 g	Fat
23%	Calories from Fat
4.1 g	Fiber
308 mg	Sodium
0 mg	Cholesterol

Cooking with Herbs

Vegetable Salad with Cilantro and Lemon

❧ ❧

1 cucumber, peeled, seeded, and sliced
2 tomatoes, halved and thinly sliced
½ sweet onion, halved and thinly sliced
½ cup thinly sliced daikon
⅓ cup sesame oil
½ cup chopped cilantro
2 tablespoons lemon zest
2 tablespoons lemon juice

PREPARATION TIME:
Less than 30 minutes

Here's a quick salad that has a nutty lemon flavor.

Combine the vegetables in a bowl and toss. Whisk together remaining ingredients and toss with salad.

Serves 4

193	Calories
1.3 g	Protein
8.1 g	Carbohydrates
18.5 g	Fat
85%	Calories from Fat
2.0 g	Fiber
14 mg	Sodium
0 mg	Cholesterol

Three-Cheese Quesadillas with Cilantro Guacamole

❧ ❧

3 avocados, peeled, halved, and pitted
3 tablespoons fresh lemon or lime juice
½ teaspoon salt
¼ teaspoon pepper
½ cup minced onion
1 tomato, halved and diced
½ cup fresh chopped cilantro
1 cup cream cheese
1 cup grated jack cheese
½ cup goat cheese
8 flour or corn tortillas

PREPARATION TIME:
Less than 30 minutes

This mixture of cheeses is delicious. I like to make these for lunch occasionally.

Mash the avocados in a bowl, then mix well with the lemon juice, salt, pepper, onion, tomato, and cilantro. Divide the cream cheese among four tortillas and spread to cover. Sprinkle equal portions of jack cheese and goat cheese over each, then place remaining tortillas on top. Heat a griddle or skillet and warm on both sides until cheese melts. Top with guacamole.

Makes 4 quesadillas

1026	Calories
32.2 g	Protein
76.5 g	Carbohydrates
66.2 g	Fat
58%	Calories from Fat
10.4 g	Fiber
835 mg	Sodium
100 mg	Cholesterol

Cooking with Herbs

Tomatoes and Avocados with Cilantro

3 ripe tomatoes, quartered
1 large avocado, diced
1 tablespoon minced
   cilantro
2 teaspoons lime juice
3 tablespoons extra-virgin
   olive oil
   Dash hot pepper sauce
¼ teaspoon salt

PREPARATION TIME:
Less than 30 minutes

Simple, quick, delicious, and colorful. A great summer salad.

Halve the tomato quarters, then toss with the avocado and cilantro. Mix remaining ingredients together, then pour over salad and toss again.

Serves 4

186 Calories
1.7 g Protein
7.5 g Carbohydrates
17.9 g Fat
86% Calories from Fat
2.1 g Fiber
149 mg Sodium
0 mg Cholesterol

Lentil Stew with Cilantro

ॐ ॐ

2 cups split lentils
1 teaspoon good-quality
    curry powder
4 cups water
2 tablespoons vegetable
    oil
1 onion, chopped
1 jalapeño, seeded and
    minced
3 tablespoons fresh grated
    ginger
1½ cups fresh chopped
    cilantro
2 tablespoons lime juice
1 tablespoon lime zest

PREPARATION TIME:
Less than 1 hour

This is spicy and flavorful, and good with herb bread.

Place the lentils and curry powder in a saucepan, add water, and bring to a boil. Cover and simmer until tender, about 25 minutes. Meanwhile, sauté the onion, pepper, and ginger in oil until onion is soft, about 7 minutes. Stir the onion mixture into the beans, then add cilantro, lime juice, and zest.

Serves 4

421	Calories
28.2 g	Protein
62.5 g	Carbohydrates
8.2 g	Fat
17%	Calories from Fat
12.3 g	Fiber
33 mg	Sodium
0 mg	Cholesterol

Cooking with Herbs

Herbed Chicken with Orange Salsa

❧ ❧

4 tablespoons fresh herbs
(thyme, rosemary, dried
basil, dill, sage)
2 tablespoons olive oil
2 whole boneless, skinless
chicken breasts, halved
½ cup dry white wine
3 green onions, chopped
1 clove finely chopped
garlic
¼ cup chopped red pepper
¼ cup chopped green
pepper
1 orange, peeled and
chopped
1 tablespoon fresh chopped
cilantro

PREPARATION TIME:
Less than 30 minutes

This is a favorite of mine, passed on to me from Wendy Kreutner. In the summer, I grill the chicken and serve it with a salad.

Combine the herbs with the olive oil, then rub on chicken breasts. Grill or fry the chicken until done. Meanwhile, cook the onion, garlic, scallion, and peppers in the white wine until just soft, about 5 minutes over low heat. Add orange and cilantro until warm. Remove from heat and pour over chicken.

Serves 4

243	Calories
27.4 g	Protein
6.4 g	Carbohydrates
10.0 g	Fat
37%	Calories from Fat
1.4 g	Fiber
67 mg	Sodium
73 mg	Cholesterol

Avocado Soup with Coriander Cream

2 ripe avocados, seeded
1 cup vegetable stock
$\frac{1}{2}$ cup half-and-half
Fresh ground pepper
$\frac{1}{2}$ cup plus $\frac{1}{8}$ cup sour cream
$\frac{1}{8}$ cup plain yogurt
1 clove garlic, minced
$\frac{1}{2}$ jalapeño, seeded and chopped
1 cup fresh chopped cilantro

PREPARATION TIME:
Less than 30 minutes
(plus chilling time)

You can be a little artistic with this and create a design on the soup as you drizzle the cream. Delicious in spring or summer.

Combine the avocados, stock, half-and-half, pepper, and $\frac{1}{2}$ cup of sour cream in a blender and purée. Chill for at least 45 minutes. Combine the yogurt, garlic, jalapeño, and cilantro in a blender and purée. Drizzle over the chilled soup; top with a dash of paprika if desired.

Serves 4 to 6

178	Calories
3.2 g	Protein
7.1 g	Carbohydrates
16.4 g	Fat
82%	Calories from Fat
1.4 g	Fiber
49 mg	Sodium
16 mg	Cholesterol

Cooking with Herbs

Cilantro Sauce

2 cups packed cilantro
⅓ cup water
1 teaspoon honey
2 serranos, seeded
½ teaspoon ginger
1 tablespoon lemon juice
2 teaspoons pine nuts

PREPARATION TIME:
Less than 30 minutes

This is a variation on a traditional Indian chutney. I also use it with Mexican foods. Serve in a bowl for dipping, or alongside spicy foods.

Place all ingredients in a blender or food processor and purée.

Makes about 2 cups (1 tablespoon per serving)

2	Calories
0.1 g	Protein
0.4 g	Carbohydrates
0.1 g	Fat
41%	Calories from Fat
0.1 g	Fiber
2 mg	Sodium
0 mg	Cholesterol

Sweet 'n' Square

❧ ❧

1½ cups flour
1 teaspoon baking powder
½ teaspoon salt
½ cup butter, softened
½ cup sugar
2 eggs, separated
½ teaspoon vanilla
½ teaspoon ground
    coriander
1 cup brown sugar
1 cup chopped hazelnuts

PREPARATION TIME:
Less than 30 minutes
(plus baking time)

These cookies delight children—both the making and the eating.

Preheat oven to 350 degrees. Lightly grease a cookie sheet. In a bowl, sift the flour with the baking powder and salt, then sift a second time and set aside. In another bowl, cream the butter, then add sugar and egg yolks and blend well. Add vanilla and coriander, then add flour mixture a little at a time to form a dough.

Turn out onto a floured surface. Press into ½-inch thickness on the cookie sheet. Beat egg whites until stiff, gradually adding the brown sugar. Fold in hazelnuts, then spread over the dough. Bake until brown, about 20 minutes. Remove from oven, then cut into squares.

Makes about 3 dozen cookies

101 Calories
1.3 g Protein
13.2 g Carbohydrates
5.0 g Fat
44% Calories from Fat
0.3 g Fiber
73 mg Sodium
20 mg Cholesterol

Blueberry Fruit Sauce

✿ ✿

1 cup blueberries
1 cup chopped honeydew
2 tablespoons honey
½ teaspoon ground
    coriander
1 teaspoon lemon zest
1 tablespoon lemon juice

PREPARATION TIME:
Less than 30 minutes

This quick sauce is not only good on desserts, but also with vegetable-fruit salad mixes and grilled chicken.

Place all in a food processor or blender and purée. Chill.

Makes about 2 cups (¼ cup per serving)

47	Calories
0.4 g	Protein
12.0 g	Carbohydrates
0.2 g	Fat
3%	Calories from Fat
1.1 g	Fiber
5 mg	Sodium
0 mg	Cholesterol

CUMIN

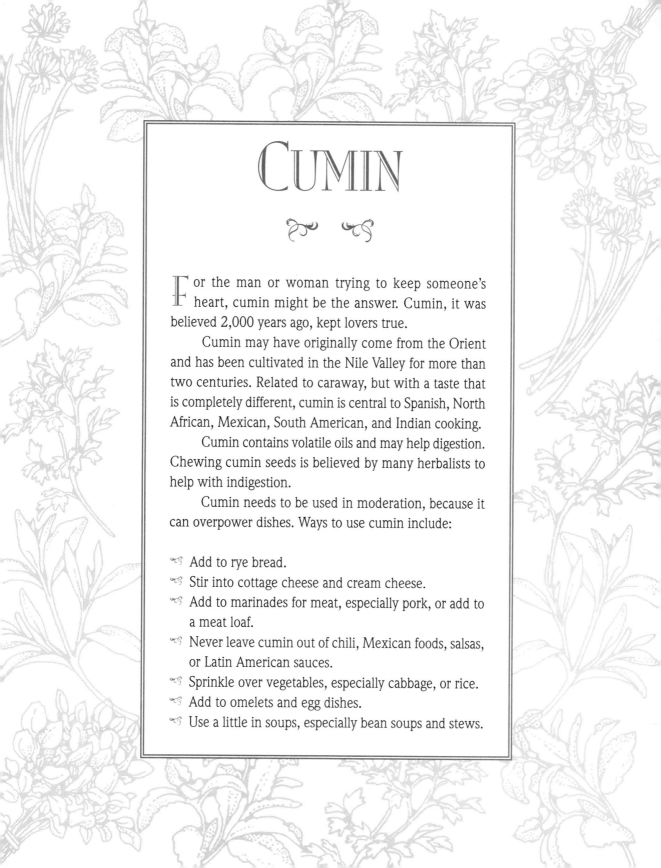

For the man or woman trying to keep someone's heart, cumin might be the answer. Cumin, it was believed 2,000 years ago, kept lovers true.

Cumin may have originally come from the Orient and has been cultivated in the Nile Valley for more than two centuries. Related to caraway, but with a taste that is completely different, cumin is central to Spanish, North African, Mexican, South American, and Indian cooking.

Cumin contains volatile oils and may help digestion. Chewing cumin seeds is believed by many herbalists to help with indigestion.

Cumin needs to be used in moderation, because it can overpower dishes. Ways to use cumin include:

- Add to rye bread.
- Stir into cottage cheese and cream cheese.
- Add to marinades for meat, especially pork, or add to a meat loaf.
- Never leave cumin out of chili, Mexican foods, salsas, or Latin American sauces.
- Sprinkle over vegetables, especially cabbage, or rice.
- Add to omelets and egg dishes.
- Use a little in soups, especially bean soups and stews.

Jicama Bean Salad with Chipotle Vinaigrette

꙰ ꙰

1 cup jicama, peeled and
   diced
1 sweet red pepper, seeded
   and diced
1 (16-ounce) can or 2 cups
   cooked black beans,
   drained and rinsed
1 (16-ounce) can or 2 cups
   cooked chickpeas,
   drained and rinsed
½ sweet onion, thinly sliced
⅓ cup fresh chopped parsley
1 tablespoon fresh lime
   juice
½ teaspoon cumin
1 tablespoon balsamic
   vinegar
2 teaspoons vegetable oil
1 chipotle chile in adobo
   sauce

PREPARATION TIME:
Less than 30 minutes

*Chipotle chiles come canned in adobo sauce. This salad is
wonderful on its own, or with Mexican foods.*

Toss the jicama, pepper, beans, chickpeas, onion, and parsley
together in a bowl. In a separate bowl, combine the lime juice,
cumin, and vinegar. Whisk in the oil, then process in a blender
with the chile in adobo sauce. Pour over salad, toss, and chill.

Serves 4 to 6

208	Calories
9.5 g	Protein
37.0 g	Carbohydrates
2.9 g	Fat
12%	Calories from Fat
3.2 g	Fiber
567 mg	Sodium
0 mg	Cholesterol

Cooking with Herbs

Carrots and Oranges and Cumin

❧ ❧

1½ pounds carrots, cut into
   pieces
1 orange, peeled and
   diced
1 tablespoon olive oil
½ teaspoon cumin
1 scallion, minced

PREPARATION TIME:
Less than 30 minutes

I like to mix fruit with vegetables for side dishes. This is good with poultry and other dishes.

Steam the carrots until done, 6 to 8 minutes. Remove to a bowl and toss with remaining ingredients.

Serves 4

124	Calories
2.3 g	Protein
22.0 g	Carbohydrates
3.8 g	Fat
27%	Calories from Fat
3.4 g	Fiber
114 mg	Sodium
0 mg	Cholesterol

Chicken with Chile–Yogurt Sauce

꩜ ꩜

2 tablespoons vegetable oil
1 red (or yellow) onion,
   finely chopped
$\frac{1}{4}$ teaspoon cumin
2 tablespoons good-quality
   chile powder
$\frac{1}{4}$ teaspoon cinnamon
$\frac{1}{2}$ teaspoon salt
$\frac{1}{2}$ cup plain yogurt
2 whole skinless chicken
   breasts, halved (boned
   if desired)

PREPARATION TIME:
Less than 30 minutes

This sauce is mild enough for children, or you can make it spicier by adding $\frac{1}{4}$ teaspoon cayenne to the chile powder.

Place onion in vegetable oil over medium heat. Add spices and stir frequently for 5 minutes. Place the onion mixture into a blender; add yogurt and purée. Sauté the chicken in the same skillet. Pour sauce on top or to the side and serve.

Serves 4

232	Calories
29.8 g	Protein
7.1 g	Carbohydrates
9.3 g	Fat
35%	Calories from Fat
1.4 g	Fiber
404 mg	Sodium
69 mg	Cholesterol

Cooking with Herbs

Southwest Stew

୧୨ ୨୧

4 new potatoes, diced

3 tablespoons vegetable or
   olive oil

1 red bell pepper, diced

1 green bell pepper, diced

3 cloves garlic, minced

1 tablespoon ground
   cumin

2 tablespoons good-quality
   chile powder

1 (28-ounce) can stewed
   tomatoes

3 cups cooked black
   beans, rinsed and
   drained

3 tablespoons fresh
   minced cilantro

PREPARATION TIME:
Less than 30 minutes

I may be in the Northwest, but I grew up in the Southwest and still love the flavors of the region. Serve this with a salad and tortillas.

Cook potatoes in boiling water until barely softened, about 10 minutes, then drain under cool water to stop the cooking. Heat oil and sauté the peppers 4 minutes; add garlic, cumin, and chile powder and stir to blend. Add potatoes, tomatoes, and black beans and simmer until the potato is tender, about 12 minutes, adding a little water as needed. Stir in cilantro and simmer another 2 minutes.

Serves 4

454	Calories
16.9 g	Protein
72.7 g	Carbohydrates
12.7 g	Fat
25%	Calories from Fat
10.0 g	Fiber
573 mg	Sodium
0 mg	Cholesterol

Corn and Black Bean Salad

1 tablespoon cider vinegar
2 teaspoons lime juice
1 small clove garlic,
    minced
½ teaspoon cumin
¼ teaspoon salt
   Dash hot pepper sauce
¼ cup extra-virgin olive oil
4 cups (about 2 cans)
    cooked black beans,
    drained and rinsed
⅓ cup seeded and diced
    red bell pepper
1 cup cooked corn
1½ cups diced jicama
¼ cup chopped cilantro

PREPARATION TIME:
Less than 30 minutes

Cumin is great with fresh ingredients, though used infrequently. I add it to my salsas, and in this dish, a salad.

Combine vinegar, lime juice, garlic, cumin, salt, and hot pepper sauce. Whisk in olive oil; set aside. Combine remaining ingredients in a bowl, then toss with the dressing.

Serves 4 to 6

269	Calories
11.3 g	Protein
36.3 g	Carbohydrates
9.9 g	Fat
33%	Calories from Fat
5.8 g	Fiber
95 mg	Sodium
0 mg	Cholesterol

Curried Chicken Salad

⁊ ⧙

1/3 cup mayonnaise
1/4 cup plain yogurt
2 teaspoons lime juice
1/2 teaspoon *each* cumin,
   turmeric, cardamom,
   and coriander
1/4 teaspoon *each* ground
   cloves and cinnamon
1 teaspoon freshly grated
   ginger
1 1/2 cups cooked chicken,
   cubed
1 stalk celery, chopped
1 apple, cored and cubed
1/4 cup raisins
1/4 cup cashews or walnuts

PREPARATION TIME:
Less than 30 minutes
(plus chilling time)

If you have a good-quality curry powder on hand, you can substitute 2 1/2 teaspoons for the curry spices (see curry powder in the Basic Recipes section).

Combine mayonnaise, yogurt, lime juice, and spices and mix well. Place remaining ingredients in a bowl and toss. Add dressing, and toss well to coat. Refrigerate at least 1 hour.

Serves 4 to 6

219	Calories
12.1 g	Protein
12.2 g	Carbohydrates
14.2 g	Fat
58%	Calories from Fat
1.1 g	Fiber
108 mg	Sodium
34 mg	Cholesterol

Orange Cumin Chicken Tostadas

෨~ ᓂ

2 boneless, skinless chicken
   breasts
2 teaspoons ground cumin
¾ cup orange juice
1 clove garlic, minced
⅛ teaspoon cayenne
6 corn tortillas
   Vegetable oil
   Shredded lettuce
   Sliced tomato

PREPARATION TIME:
Less than 1 hour

Orange and cumin are a natural marriage. These make a delicious, healthful dinner.

Dice the chicken and combine with cumin, orange juice, garlic, and cayenne. Mix well, cover, and chill for 30 minutes, or up to 6 hours. Grill over a barbecue or cook in a little oil until cooked. In a skillet, heat enough oil to cover the pan. Place one tortilla in the oil and cook over medium heat for a minute or so on each side, until crisp. Dry and repeat with all of the tortillas. Place lettuce on top of the tortilla, add chicken and tomato, then top with salsa or sour cream or yogurt if desired.

Makes 6 tostadas

195	Calories
20.2 g	Protein
19.3 g	Carbohydrates
3.5 g	Fat
16%	Calories from Fat
2.3 g	Fiber
102 mg	Sodium
49 mg	Cholesterol

Tangy Chicken Marinade

2 boneless, skinless chicken
   breasts
3 cloves garlic
2 teaspoons freshly grated
   ginger
$1/2$ teaspoon ground cumin
$1/4$ teaspoon turmeric
$1/4$ teaspoon cardamom
   Scant $1/8$ teaspoon
   cayenne
$3/4$ teaspoon salt
$1/4$ teaspoon pepper
2 tablespoons white vinegar
2 tablespoons olive oil or
   butter (optional)

PREPARATION TIME:
Less than 30 minutes
(plus marinating time)

*The combination of spices gives this chicken a tangy flavor.
Serve with a rice dish.*

Rinse and pat the chicken dry, and cut each breast in half. Mix
all ingredients (except olive oil) together and spread over the
chicken, turning occasionally as it marinates 45 minutes. Heat
oil in a skillet, or prepare a grill. Cook chicken about 4 minutes
on each side, or until done.

Serves 4

137	Calories
27.5 g	Protein
1.9 g	Carbohydrates
1.6 g	Fat
10%	Calories from Fat
0.1 g	Fiber
477 mg	Sodium
68 mg	Cholesterol

Spicy Chicken Tacos

⁓ ⁓

¾ pound boneless, skinless chicken
1 tablespoon vegetable oil, plus extra for cooking tortillas
1 tablespoon chile powder
1 teaspoon ground cumin
½ teaspoon dried oregano
8 corn tortillas
1 cucumber, peeled, seeded, and diced
¼ sweet onion, diced
2 tablespoons chopped cilantro

PREPARATION TIME:
Less than 1 hour

I like the cool cucumber taste with the spicy meat. You might add a mild salsa to these—or add anything you like to put on tacos.

Poach or grill the chicken until cooked. Cool and shred into bite-sized pieces. Warm oil in a skillet and add chile powder, cumin, and oregano. Stir chicken pieces in, coat, and cook until warmed, about 5 minutes. In a separate skillet, heat a little oil and warm the tortillas, one at a time, until soft, about 2 minutes each side. Drain on paper towels. Place a portion of the chicken in each tortilla and add cucumber and onion. Sprinkle with cilantro.

Makes 8 tacos

152	Calories
11.8 g	Protein
15.8 g	Carbohydrates
4.4 g	Fat
26%	Calories from Fat
2.3 g	Fiber
88 mg	Sodium
27 mg	Cholesterol

Cooking with Herbs

DILL

Dill is native to the Mediterranean and Black Sea regions. At one time dill was thought of as a pain killer. In colonial days dill cakes were given to teething babies. For centuries dill water was considered a treatment for colic in Europe and many colic remedies still contain dill.

Herbalists recommend dill for flatulence, as an aid to digestion, and to help increase the milk supply for nursing mothers. It may also help to increase the appetite.

Here are some ways to add dill to your diet:

- Great with fish; add to sauces or to liquid in which fish is cooked.
- Sprinkle on meats, especially lamb, just before they are done.
- Add to vegetable salads, vinaigrettes and French dressings, green salads, potato salad, coleslaw, and seafood salads.
- Sprinkle on soups, especially potato.
- Add a little to tomato juice.
- Mix dill into cream cheese or butter. Buttered dill is great on vegetables.
- Add to vegetable dishes. I frequently add a touch of dill to sautéed zucchini. Add to beets, turnips, squash, green beans, and more.

Oregon Salad

4 cups mesclun or other mixed greens

½ red bell pepper, very thinly sliced

3 tablespoons raspberry vinegar

1 teaspoon freshly chopped dill, or ½ teaspoon dried

¼ teaspoon salt, or to taste

¼ teaspoon pepper, or to taste

6 tablespoons extra-virgin olive oil

¾ cup toasted hazelnuts, coarsely chopped

½ cup gorgonzola or blue cheese, coarsely crumbled

PREPARATION TIME:
Less than 30 minutes

This salad is particularly good with the variety of greens in mesclun. If you mix your own greens, use as many different types as possible.

Combine the mesclun and bell pepper. In a small bowl, mix the vinegar and spices, then whisk in the olive oil to blend. Toss with mixed greens, sprinkle on hazelnuts and cheese, and serve.

Serves 4 to 6

265	Calories
4.2 g	Protein
6.8 g	Carbohydrates
26.0 g	Fat
88%	Calories from Fat
1.7 g	Fiber
225 mg	Sodium
7 mg	Cholesterol

Warm Potato Salad with Dill

❦ ❧

2 pounds new potatoes
1 teaspoon salt
½ teaspoon pepper
4 green onions, chopped
1 tablespoon fresh dill, chopped
¾ cup sour cream
2 tablespoons milk
¼ cup plain yogurt

PREPARATION TIME:
Less than 1 hour

I like dill in potato salads, both cold and warm. This is a simple and satisfying combination.

Scrub the potatoes and place in a pot of water. Bring to a boil and cook until tender, about 15 minutes. Drain and leave until cool enough to handle. Dice the potatoes (peeled or unpeeled) and place into a bowl. Add the salt, pepper, onions, and dill. Combine the sour cream, milk, and yogurt. Stir into the potatoes and toss.

Serves 4 to 6

191	Calories
4.4 g	Protein
32.2 g	Carbohydrates
5.3 g	Fat
25%	Calories from Fat
6.1 g	Fiber
384 mg	Sodium
11 mg	Cholesterol

Dilled Bean and Sweet Pepper Salad

❧ ❧

¾ pound green beans,
    trimmed and halved
1 red bell pepper, cut into
    matchsticks
1 carrot, sliced
1 tablespoon Dijon mustard
1 teaspoon sour cream or
    yogurt
1 teaspoon lemon juice
1 tablespoon balsamic
    vinegar
¼ teaspoon pepper
1 teaspoon dill, minced

PREPARATION TIME:
Less than 30 minutes

Serve chilled or at room temperature. It's perfect for a picnic and is very colorful on the plate.

Blanch the beans in boiling water for about 5 minutes, until just cooked. Rinse well in cold water, then toss with pepper and carrot. Combine remaining ingredients and whisk well. Pour over vegetables and toss.

Serves 4

35	Calories
1.2 g	Protein
6.5 g	Carbohydrates
0.8 g	Fat
20%	Calories from Fat
1.5 g	Fiber
219 mg	Sodium
0 mg	Cholesterol

Cream of Potato, Lemon, and Dill Soup

※ ※

3 tablespoons butter
3 sweet onions
3 potatoes, peeled and
 cubed
½ teaspoon pepper
6 cups vegetable or chicken
 stock
½ cup cream
⅓ cup lemon juice
4 tablespoons finely minced
 fresh dill

PREPARATION TIME:
Less than 30 minutes
(plus cooking time)

If you really like lemon add a little zest to this when you stir in the lemon juice.

Melt the butter in a large pot. Halve and then thinly slice the onion and add to the butter. Sauté until soft. Add potatoes, season with pepper, and sauté 5 minutes, stirring frequently to prevent the butter from browning.

Add stock, bring to a boil, and simmer, covered, 1 hour, or until potatoes are tender. Whisk together the cream and lemon juice and set aside. Purée the soup in batches and return to the pot. Stir in the cream and lemon and warm, but do not boil. Sprinkle each serving with dill.

Serves 4 to 6

175	Calories
3.1 g	Protein
22.5 g	Carbohydrates
8.6 g	Fat
44%	Calories from Fat
2.0 g	Fiber
77 mg	Sodium
24 mg	Cholesterol

Simple Summer Vegetables

⚬⚬ ⚬⚬

3 tablespoons olive oil
1 large sweet onion, cut in half, thinly sliced
2 zucchini, sliced
4 to 5 mushrooms, sliced
1 tablespoon fresh chopped dill, or 1 1/2 teaspoons dried
1 tablespoon fresh chopped thyme, or 1 1/2 teaspoons dried
1 clove garlic
1 cup Parmesan cheese

PREPARATION TIME:
Less than 30 minutes

I often make this Provençal-style dish. Cook the vegetables to your taste.

Sauté onion in the olive oil about 3 minutes. Add zucchini, mushrooms, dill, and thyme and sauté another 6 or 7 minutes.

Meanwhile, cut the garlic clove in half and use it to rub the bottom of a casserole dish. Spread the zucchini and onion mix in the casserole dish, spread the Parmesan on top, and broil until the cheese has melted completely.

Serves 4 to 6

139	Calories
6.6 g	Protein
4.3 g	Carbohydrates
10.9 g	Fat
70%	Calories from Fat
1.0 g	Fiber
251 mg	Sodium
11 mg	Cholesterol

Cooking with Herbs

Vegetables with Dill Sauce

2 small zucchini, sliced
½ sweet onion, thinly sliced
2 vine-ripened tomatoes,
    sliced
1 cucumber, peeled,
    seeded, and sliced
2 tablespoons fresh dill,
    minced
1 cup plain yogurt
1 teaspoon fresh lime or
    lemon juice
1 scallion, minced
½ teaspoon sugar
   Salt and white pepper

PREPARATION TIME:
Less than 30 minutes

This is a refreshing summer salad or vegetable side dish. It goes well with fish dishes.

Place the vegetables in a bowl and mix. Combine remaining ingredients and blend well. Place a spoonful (more to taste) on each serving of vegetables.

Serves 4 to 6

48	Calories
3.4 g	Protein
8.7 g	Carbohydrates
0.3 g	Fat
6%	Calories from Fat
1.6 g	Fiber
36 mg	Sodium
1 mg	Cholesterol

Halibut in Lemon–Dill Cream Sauce

2 pounds halibut steaks or
    fillets
2 tablespoons lemon juice
2 tablespoons fresh dill
¼ cup plain yogurt
1 tablespoon honey
⅛ cup milk

PREPARATION TIME:
Less than 30 minutes

You can use this sauce on cod, red snapper, pollock, sword-fish, or another fish of your choice. Serve with rice or a salad.

Broil or grill the fish until done, 4 to 5 minutes per side. Meanwhile, combine lemon juice and dill. In a separate bowl, combine the yogurt, honey, and milk. Stir into the lemon-dill mixture, and pour over cooked fish.

Serves 4

262	Calories
45.2 g	Protein
6.3 g	Carbohydrates
5.0 g	Fat
17%	Calories from Fat
0.0 g	Fiber
129 mg	Sodium
68 mg	Cholesterol

Cooking with Herbs

Cold Cucumber Soup

2 cucumbers, peeled,
  seeded, and chopped
1½ cups cottage cheese
¾ cup plain yogurt
1 green onion, minced
2 tablespoons fresh
  minced dill

PREPARATION TIME:
Less than 30 minutes
(plus chilling time)

This simple refreshing salad is great with spicy foods and barbecues.

Combine all ingredients in a food processor and blend until smooth. Chill until cold. (You may add ¾ cup crushed ice and reprocess rather than chilling.)

Serves 4

121	Calories
15.0 g	Protein
11.0 g	Carbohydrates
1.9 g	Fat
14%	Calories from Fat
1.6 g	Fiber
381 mg	Sodium
8 mg	Cholesterol

Lime–Dill Coleslaw

¼ red cabbage, shredded
¼ green cabbage, shredded
2 cups thinly sliced daikon
3 tablespoons fresh
    minced dill
2 tablespoons lime juice
1 tablespoon white wine
    vinegar
5 tablespoons extra-virgin
    olive oil

PREPARATION TIME:
Less than 30 minutes

The crisp taste of the cabbage and daikon, mixed with a simple dill and lemon flavoring, is very refreshing. Great with spicy foods.

Mix cabbage and daikon in a bowl. Whisk remaining ingredients well, then toss with salad.

Serves 4

180 Calories
1.4 g Protein
7.7 g Carbohydrates
17.1 g Fat
85% Calories from Fat
2.0 g Fiber
22 mg Sodium
0 mg Cholesterol

Cooking with Herbs

Shrimp, Celery, and Dill Salad

20 to 25 medium shrimp,
    cooked
3 stalks celery, thinly sliced
½ cup olive oil
    Juice of ½ lemon
    Zest of ½ lemon
3 tablespoons fresh
    chopped dill
¼ teaspoon salt
¼ teaspoon pepper

PREPARATION TIME:
Less than 30 minutes

This simple dressing allows the flavor of the shrimp to shine.

Combine the shrimp and celery in a bowl and mix. Combine remaining ingredients and whisk well, then pour over shrimp and celery and toss.

Serves 4

357	Calories
23.9 g	Protein
2.4 g	Carbohydrates
28.3 g	Fat
71%	Calories from Fat
0.5 g	Fiber
412 mg	Sodium
221 mg	Cholesterol

Dilled Tomato Soup

❧ ☙

2 cloves garlic, minced

2 tablespoons fresh chopped dill

1 cup cucumber, seeded and diced

5 cups peeled, seeded, and puréed tomatoes, or fresh tomato juice

Juice of $1/2$ lemon

$1/2$ small sweet onion, finely chopped

$1/3$ cup fresh chopped cilantro

PREPARATION TIME:
Less than 30 minutes
(plus chilling time)

Dill is good in tomato juice and in tomato soup. This soup is very refreshing on a hot day.

Stir all ingredients together and chill for an hour or more.

Serves 4 to 6

43	Calories
1.7 g	Protein
9.6 g	Carbohydrates
0.6 g	Fat
12%	Calories from Fat
2.5 g	Fiber
17 mg	Sodium
0 mg	Cholesterol

Cooking with Herbs

Dilled Mustard

੭৶ ৵੧

2 tablespoons Dijon
  mustard
1 tablespoon cider vinegar
2 teaspoons lemon juice
2 tablespoons honey
¼ cup vegetable oil
1½ tablespoons fresh
  chopped dill

PREPARATION TIME:
Less than 30 minutes

Dilled mustard is a traditional Scandinavian accompaniment for fish. Although it is available in jars, mustard made with fresh dill is much more flavorful. This doesn't make a lot of mustard, but you don't need a lot to serve with fish. You might try it as an appetizer with fresh vegetables.

Combine all ingredients (except the oil and dill) in a bowl. Slowly add the oil and whisk constantly to blend. Stir in dill.

Makes about ³/₄ cup (2 tablespoons per serving)

114	Calories
0.4 g	Protein
6.2 g	Carbohydrates
10.0 g	Fat
79%	Calories from Fat
0.0 g	Fiber
132 mg	Sodium
0 mg	Cholesterol

Halibut with Mushroom–Dill Wine Sauce

૨૦ ૯૬

⅓ cup chicken stock
½ pound mushrooms, thinly sliced
3 small shallots, peeled and minced
1¼ cups dry white wine
1½ tablespoons fresh, finely chopped dill
1 tablespoon cornstarch, dissolved in 1 tablespoon water
Halibut steaks or fillets

PREPARATION TIME:
Less than 30 minutes

You can substitute swordfish, sole, or even a turkey burger for the halibut.

Place the stock in a saucepan, then add the mushrooms and shallots. Cover and cook over medium-low heat for 8 to 9 minutes, until mushrooms turn dark. Add wine and bring to a boil. Reduce heat and simmer, uncovered, 10 minutes. Turn heat to low, add dill and cornstarch mixture, and cook, stirring constantly, for a minute, or until thickened.

Broil or barbecue the halibut, then pour sauce over.

Makes enough sauce for 6 to 8 servings

251	Calories
43.3 g	Protein
3.7 g	Carbohydrates
4.8 g	Fat
17%	Calories from Fat
0.5 g	Fiber
117 mg	Sodium
65 mg	Cholesterol

FENNEL

Fennel is a member of the carrot family and a native of southern Europe. In U.S. markets we see common fennel, but there is also a sweet fennel called Florence fennel (or finocchio) and an Italian fennel called carosella.

Fennel, with its faint licorice scent, is among the oldest of herbs. Pliny believed that before serpents cast off their skins they ate fennel. The root has been used as a medicine since ancient times. The Greeks believed fennel controlled weight gain and in the Middle Ages fennel was thought to control weight and help eyesight. (Many herbalists still recommend it as an eyewash for tired eyes.)

All of the fennel plant is edible. The bulb, or root, is good raw or cooked; the seeds are useful to spice up many dishes; and the leaves, similar to dill, can be chopped and added to salads. Fennel is useful for colic in babies, and for both indigestion and heartburn in adults.

Fennel is good in many dishes:

- Sprinkle seeds on breads and rolls before baking.
- Add seeds or sliced bulb to omelets.
- Thinly slice bulb or leaves and add to salads.
- Use fennel with pork dishes.
- Sprinkle fennel seeds over soups, or add sliced fennel to vegetable soup.
- Use seeds in liquid in which fish is cooked, or add to fish sauces.
- Add to many Italian dishes, including tomato sauces.

Fennel with Parmesan

꩜ ꩜

2 fennel bulbs, trimmed
   and halved
½ cup chicken broth or
   water
3 tablespoons Parmesan
2 tablespoons bread crumbs
½ teaspoon coriander
¼ teaspoon pepper

PREPARATION TIME:
Less than 1 hour

This easy dish is a nice accompaniment to meat or fish entrées.

Preheat oven to 375 degrees. Oil a baking dish and place the fennel, cut side down, in the dish. Pour in the broth or water, cover tightly with foil, and bake 40 minutes, until fennel is soft.

Combine remaining ingredients in a bowl. Turn the fennel over, sprinkle with the bread mixture, and bake uncovered until crumbs are browned.

Serves 4

68	Calories
3.7 g	Protein
11.3 g	Carbohydrates
1.6 g	Fat
20%	Calories from Fat
2.0 g	Fiber
164 mg	Sodium
3 mg	Cholesterol

Fennel Daikon Salad with Lemon Vinaigrette

2 large fennel bulbs,
    trimmed, cored, and
    thinly sliced
1 cucumber, peeled,
    seeded, and sliced
1½ cups daikon, halved and
    sliced
2 tablespoons white wine
    vinegar
2 teaspoons lemon juice
1 tablespoon finely
    minced shallots
6 tablespoons extra-virgin
    olive oil

PREPARATION TIME:
Less than 30 minutes

Slice the fennel very thin, and mince the shallots very fine so that neither flavor overwhelms this salad.

Combine the fennel, cucumber, and daikon in a bowl. Whisk together the remaining ingredients, then toss with the salad ingredients.

Serves 4 to 6

161 Calories
1.6 g Protein
10.0 g Carbohydrates
13.8 g Fat
77% Calories from Fat
2.2 g Fiber
54 mg Sodium
0 mg Cholesterol

Brown Rice with Fennel

2 tablespoons butter
1 tablespoon olive oil
1 small onion, minced
6 mushrooms, sliced
1 small fennel bulb, chopped
1 cup brown rice
3 cups stock or water

PREPARATION TIME:
Less than 30 minutes
(plus cooking time)

I like to serve this dish with simply cooked fish. I prepare the seafood while the rice cooks.

Heat butter and oil and add onion, then cook 3 minutes. Add mushrooms, fennel, and rice and mix to coat well. Add stock and bring to a boil. Cover, reduce heat, and cook until liquid has been absorbed, about 50 minutes.

Serves 4

292	Calories
5.5 g	Protein
43.4 g	Carbohydrates
11.1 g	Fat
34%	Calories from Fat
3.0 g	Fiber
94 mg	Sodium
17 mg	Cholesterol

Cooking with Herbs

Spaghetti in Tomato Sauce with Fennel

❧ ❧

2 tablespoons extra-virgin
   olive oil
1 large fennel bulb,
   julienned
½ small onion, minced
1 (15-ounce) can tomatoes,
   with juice
½ cup water
2 cloves garlic, minced
½ teaspoon dried thyme
½ teaspoon dried marjoram
1 bay leaf
½ teaspoon pepper
½ cup dry red wine
¼ cup fresh torn basil, or
   ⅛ cup dried
¼ cup fresh chopped parsley
2 tablespoons butter or oil
1 pound spaghetti or
   other pasta

PREPARATION TIME:
Less than 1 hour
(plus cooking time)

Fennel adds its anise-like flavor to this tomato sauce. You can make this a meat sauce if you like; sauté the ground meat before adding the fennel and onion.

Sauté the fennel bulb in oil in a large pot for 10 minutes; add onion and sauté another 5 minutes. Add tomatoes, water, garlic, thyme, marjoram, bay leaf, and pepper and bring to a boil. Reduce heat and simmer, stirring occasionally, for 1 hour. Add wine, basil, and parsley and cook 30 minutes longer. Meanwhile, cook pasta according to package directions, drain, then toss with sauce.

Serves 4 to 6

413 Calories
11.6 g Protein
67.9 g Carbohydrates
10.1 g Fat
22% Calories from Fat
4.7 g Fiber
256 mg Sodium
11 mg Cholesterol

Fennel–Beet Borscht

1 cup chopped fennel
2 carrots, finely chopped
3 beets, peeled, trimmed, and diced
½ onion, minced
½ teaspoon fennel seeds
½ teaspoon allspice
1 cup shredded cabbage
1 tablespoon wine vinegar
1 cup grated cucumber

PREPARATION TIME:
Less than 1 hour

This bright colored soup is a winter favorite when root vegetables are the order of the day.

Place the fennel, carrots, beets, onion, and spices in a pot and cover with water or vegetable stock. Bring to a boil and simmer 30 minutes. Stir in cabbage and vinegar and simmer another 15 minutes. Top with grated cucumber, and sour cream if desired.

Serves 4 to 6

62	Calories
2.2 g	Protein
14.0 g	Carbohydrates
0.3 g	Fat
4%	Calories from Fat
1.9 g	Fiber
89 mg	Sodium
0 mg	Cholesterol

Cooking with Herbs

Orange and Fennel Salad

2 fennel bulbs, washed, trimmed, and julienned
2 oranges, peeled and sectioned, reserving juice
⅛ cup extra-virgin olive oil
⅓ cup orange or lemon juice
Salt and pepper

PREPARATION TIME:
Less than 30 minutes

This bright salad is something I serve in the fall with pumpkin or red pepper soup.

Place fennel and oranges in a bowl. Mix remaining ingredients and pour over salad. Toss well.

Serves 4 to 6

90	Calories
1.5 g	Protein
12.3 g	Carbohydrates
4.7 g	Fat
46%	Calories from Fat
2.3 g	Fiber
41 mg	Sodium
0 mg	Cholesterol

GARLIC

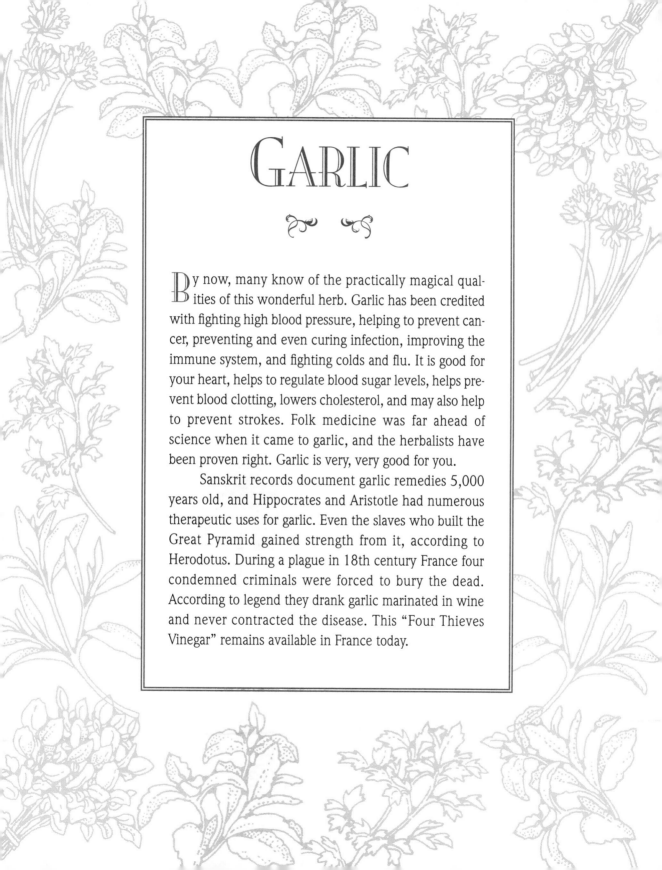

By now, many know of the practically magical qualities of this wonderful herb. Garlic has been credited with fighting high blood pressure, helping to prevent cancer, preventing and even curing infection, improving the immune system, and fighting colds and flu. It is good for your heart, helps to regulate blood sugar levels, helps prevent blood clotting, lowers cholesterol, and may also help to prevent strokes. Folk medicine was far ahead of science when it came to garlic, and the herbalists have been proven right. Garlic is very, very good for you.

Sanskrit records document garlic remedies 5,000 years old, and Hippocrates and Aristotle had numerous therapeutic uses for garlic. Even the slaves who built the Great Pyramid gained strength from it, according to Herodotus. During a plague in 18th century France four condemned criminals were forced to bury the dead. According to legend they drank garlic marinated in wine and never contracted the disease. This "Four Thieves Vinegar" remains available in France today.

Garlic's popularity as a medicinal continued to grow. Louis Pasteur noted garlic's antibiotic activity in the 19th century. During the two World Wars, garlic was applied to wounds to prevent gangrene. Researchers in the 1960s discovered that garlic helped to reduce tumors.

Herbalists now take garlic further. It has been shown to help diarrhea, dysentery, diphtheria, and works as a digestive.

Fresh garlic tastes wonderful, which is not true of garlic powder, garlic salt, preserved garlic, and limp, yellow, or green garlic that has been kept too long. Fresh garlic should be used in any recipe calling for the herb. Many who find garlic's taste too strong are probably tasting a dried version or garlic that is too old. If garlic's taste remains strong following a meal, try chewing on parsley to dissipate the flavor.

Garlic comes from southern Europe and is related to the onion and leek. Here are some ideas for using garlic:

- Rub a salad bowl or pasta bowl with a peeled and pressed clove, to give just a hint of garlic flavor.
- Add to almost any salad dressing—a must for vinaigrettes.
- Stir into butters to serve on vegetables.
- Add to casseroles, especially vegetarian.
- Sautés and stir-fries can always benefit from garlic.
- Roast until soft (it becomes sweet) and spread on bread.
- Add to soups when you sauté other vegetables.
- Add to sauces, especially vegetable-based sauces such as tomato.
- Rub on meats and vegetables before grilling.
- Bake minced garlic into bread.

Cooking with Herbs

Toasted Garlic Soup

೪⊷ ⊶೪

2 tablespoons olive oil
8 to 10 heads garlic, peeled
   and coarsely chopped
1 poblano, seeded and
   chopped
1 jalapeño, seeded and
   chopped
3 to 4 tomatoes, peeled,
   seeded, and cut into
   chunks
7 cups vegetable or chicken
   stock
½ teaspoon salt
   Grated jack or cheddar
   cheese (optional)
   Sour cream (optional)

PREPARATION TIME:
Less than 30 minutes
(plus cooking time)

*The trick to making this soup great is to toast the garlic with-
out burning it. Much more healthful than even grandmother's
chicken soup.*

Heat the oil until almost smoking. Add garlic and stir for a
minute or so, until toasted. Transfer garlic to a soup pot.
    Sauté the peppers and tomatoes in skillet for 2 minutes.
Transfer to the pot and add stock and salt. Bring to a boil and
simmer 25 minutes, until garlic is soft. Add cheese or sour cream
to each serving if desired.

Serves 4 to 6

158	Calories
5.6 g	Protein
27.9 g	Carbohydrates
5.3 g	Fat
30%	Calories from Fat
2.4 g	Fiber
319 mg	Sodium
0 mg	Cholesterol

Grilled Chicken with Gazpacho Salsa

❦

½ cucumber, peeled,
   seeded, and minced
½ green bell pepper, seeded
   and minced
½ red bell pepper, seeded
   and minced
2 tomatoes, peeled, seeded,
   and diced
2 stalks celery, minced
3 scallions, finely chopped
2 cloves garlic, minced
2 tablespoons finely
   chopped cilantro
  Juice of 1 lemon
2 tablespoons extra-virgin
   olive oil
½ teaspoon salt
½ teaspoon pepper
2 chicken breasts, skinned
   and halved
4 large flour tortillas

PREPARATION TIME:
Less than 30 minutes
(plus chill time)

This is a colorful, delicious dinner to serve to guests or family.

Place the cucumber, peppers, and tomatoes in a strainer and press to expel excess juice. Toss together the next eight ingredients and chill slightly. Grill the chicken, then cut into dice. Warm tortillas in an oven, then place chicken pieces inside. Place chilled salsa mixture in small bowl on each plate for scooping into tortilla, or spoon over chicken.

Serves 4

437	Calories
34.3 g	Protein
39.2 g	Carbohydrates
14.8 g	Fat
30%	Calories from Fat
5.5 g	Fiber
418 mg	Sodium
73 mg	Cholesterol

Cooking with Herbs

Roasted Garlic Potatoes

⤳ ⤳

1 large head garlic, top
    ¼ inch cut off
1 tablespoon olive oil
3 to 4 baking potatoes,
    peeled and quartered
3 tablespoons butter
1 cup lowfat milk

PREPARATION TIME:
Less than 1 hour

Roasted garlic is wonderful spread on bread as an appetizer, but here it's added to mashed potatoes. Garlic changes its flavor once it's roasted—it becomes sweet.

Preheat oven to 350 degrees. Drizzle the garlic head with oil, then wrap securely in foil (or place in a garlic roaster). Put into the oven and roast 30 to 40 minutes, until soft. Cool, then squeeze garlic from skins. Meanwhile, boil the potatoes until tender, about 20 minutes. Drain and mash well, then add butter and garlic and mix well. Add milk to desired consistency.

Serves 6 to 8

138	Calories
2.6 g	Protein
17.0 g	Carbohydrates
7.1 g	Fat
46%	Calories from Fat
1.1 g	Fiber
68 mg	Sodium
15 mg	Cholesterol

Fisherman's Spaghetti

❧ ❧

¼ cup extra-virgin olive oil
½ onion, chopped
3 to 4 cloves garlic, minced
1 pound tomatoes, or
    1 (16-ounce) can
¼ cup dry white wine
¼ cup fish, vegetable, or
    chicken broth
1 tablespoon fresh chopped
    marjoram, or
    1 teaspoon dried
1 tablespoon fresh chopped
    basil, or ½ teaspoon
    dried
2 tablespoons fresh
    chopped parsley
1 pound of fish, cut into
    chunks
1 pound spaghetti

PREPARATION TIME:
Less than 1 hour

This is a garlic lover's delight and a hearty fish soup. Serve with a crusty bread.

Place oil in a pot and add onion and garlic. Turn heat to medium and sauté until soft, about 8 minutes. Be careful not to burn the garlic. Add tomatoes, wine, broth, and, if using dried herbs, the marjoram and basil. Bring to a boil, reduce heat, and cook 25 minutes. If using fresh herbs, add the marjoram and basil with the parsley and cook for 5 minutes longer. Add the fish and cook another 5 minutes, or until fish is cooked.

While the sauce is simmering, cook spaghetti according to package directions. Drain and toss with the sauce.

Serves 4 to 6

463	Calories
24.5 g	Protein
64.6 g	Carbohydrates
11.2 g	Fat
21%	Calories from Fat
4.5 g	Fiber
54 mg	Sodium
33 mg	Cholesterol

Cooking with Herbs

Provençal Tian

୧୬ ୬୧

2 onions, halved and
    sliced
2 sweet peppers, red or
    green, seeded and
    sliced
1 small eggplant, peeled
    and cut into thin
    strips
5 tablespoons extra-virgin
    olive oil
5 cloves garlic, chopped
1½ teaspoons fresh
    rosemary, or
    ½ teaspoon dried
1½ teaspoons fresh thyme,
    or ½ teaspoon dried
¼ teaspoon salt
¼ teaspoon pepper
2 small zucchini, thinly
    sliced
3 tomatoes, sliced
⅓ cup grated Parmesan
    cheese

PREPARATION TIME:
Less than 30 minutes
(plus baking time)

This is a version of a popular French casserole, or tian. It's a healthful and filling dish.

Preheat oven to 375 degrees. Sauté the onions, peppers, eggplant, and 3 garlic cloves in 3 tablespoons of the oil over medium-low heat until softened, 15 to 20 minutes. Season with 2 teaspoons of the herbs, salt, and pepper. Remove the vegetables to a baking dish and top with the zucchini and tomatoes. Sprinkle with remaining herbs, garlic, and olive oil. Bake 25 minutes, sprinkle with cheese, and bake another 20 minutes.

Serves 4 to 6

172	Calories
4.0 g	Protein
11.9 g	Carbohydrates
13.0 g	Fat
68%	Calories from Fat
2.6 g	Fiber
181 mg	Sodium
4 mg	Cholesterol

Green Beans with Shallots and Garlic

1½ pounds green beans
1 tablespoon butter
2 shallots, peeled and
finely chopped
1 clove garlic, minced

PREPARATION TIME:
Less than 30 minutes

This quick dish is a good side to many entrées, especially meats.

Trim the beans and boil 3 minutes, until just cooked. Drain and rinse. Melt butter in the pot and stir in garlic. Sauté 5 minutes, stirring to prevent garlic from browning, then add the shallot and sauté another 2 minutes. Return beans to the pot and toss well.

Serves 4

89	Calories
3.2 g	Protein
14.1 g	Carbohydrates
3.5 g	Fat
35%	Calories from Fat
2.9 g	Fiber
37 mg	Sodium
8 mg	Cholesterol

Green Bean and Blackened Red Pepper Salad

☙ ❧

3 tablespoons extra-virgin olive oil

1 tablespoon balsamic vinegar

2 tablespoons chopped parsley

1 cup green beans, cut into 1-inch pieces

4 sweet red peppers, seeded and sliced into matchsticks

1 clove garlic, minced

PREPARATION TIME:
Less than 30 minutes

I have always loved blackened red peppers on the grill, but in the fall barbecuing isn't very practical in Oregon. This mix of blackened peppers and beans is a quick and colorful side dish.

Combine 1 tablespoon of the oil with the balsamic vinegar and parsley and set aside. Blanch the green beans in boiling water until just crisp-tender, 3 to 4 minutes, then rinse to stop cooking process. Pour the remaining oil in a skillet and heat almost to smoking. Carefully add peppers and sauté until they begin to blacken. Reduce heat and add garlic, stirring to prevent burning. Sauté for a minute, then add green beans to heat. Remove, with oil, to a bowl and toss with dressing.

Serves 4 to 6

84	Calories
0.9 g	Protein
5.8 g	Carbohydrates
6.9 g	Fat
74%	Calories from Fat
0.9 g	Fiber
3 mg	Sodium
0 mg	Cholesterol

Ratatouille Soup

2 tablespoons olive oil
½ onion, peeled and
    chopped
2 cloves garlic, minced
1 cup diced zucchini
½ bell pepper, diced
1 cup diced eggplant
3 tomatoes, peeled,
    seeded, and chopped
¼ cup tomato juice
2 tablespoons fresh basil,
    or 1 tablespoon dried
1 teaspoon oregano
2½ cups vegetable or
    chicken stock

PREPARATION TIME:
Less than 30 minutes

My artist friend Paul Strauch makes a great ratatouille, and this is an adaptation of his version of the classic French vegetable dish.

Place oil in a skillet and combine with onion and garlic. Sauté over medium-low heat for 3 minutes, being careful not to burn the garlic. Add zucchini, pepper, and eggplant and sauté another 7 to 8 minutes. Add the tomatoes, tomato juice, spices, and stock and bring to a boil. Cover and cook 10 minutes. Serve with Parmesan cheese, if desired.

Serves 4 to 6

71	Calories
1.4 g	Protein
7.0 g	Carbohydrates
4.8 g	Fat
60%	Calories from Fat
1.5 g	Fiber
43 mg	Sodium
0 mg	Cholesterol

Cooking with Herbs

Chicken and Zucchini with Almond Pesto

❧ ❧

½ cup almonds
½ pound farfalle (bowtie) or
   other pasta
2 zucchini, sliced
1 clove garlic, minced
⅓ cup extra-virgin olive oil
1 tablespoon white wine
   vinegar
   Dash hot pepper sauce
2 cups cubed cooked
   chicken

PREPARATION TIME:
Less than 30 minutes

This sauce won't keep, so use it right away. I poach or sauté a chicken breast and cut it into pieces, but this works well with leftover chicken as well. Vegetarians can replace the chicken with more pasta or another vegetable, if desired.

Toast the almonds in a 300 degree oven until the skins begin to crack, about 10 minutes. Cool, then finely chop by hand or in a food processor. Cook pasta according to package directions. Steam zucchini until crisp-tender, about 8 minutes.

Mix together remaining ingredients, then add the toasted almonds and mix well. Combine pasta, zucchini, and chicken and toss. Add dressing and toss well.

Serves 4

579	Calories
31.0 g	Protein
45.2 g	Carbohydrates
30.9 g	Fat
48%	Calories from Fat
6.3 g	Fiber
50 mg	Sodium
54 mg	Cholesterol

Mexican Vegetables

๛ ๖

1 tablespoon olive oil
1 onion, chopped
2 green or red peppers,
    diced
1 tablespoon minced
    jalapeño
2 cloves garlic, minced
½ teaspoon chile powder
½ teaspoon ground cumin
1 tablespoon fresh oregano
2 tomatoes, peeled and
    chopped, or
    1 (16-ounce) can
1 cup cooked black beans,
    rinsed and drained
2 tablespoons minced
    cilantro or parsley
  Juice of 1 lime
3 cups cooked rice

PREPARATION TIME:
Less than 30 minutes

This is an easy dish, and you can add other vegetables you have on hand, from broccoli to zucchini. Leftover cooked chicken also goes well in this dish.

Heat oil in a skillet and sauté the onion and peppers until soft, about 5 minutes. Add garlic, spices, tomatoes, and beans and cook over low-medium heat for another 5 minutes, or until warmed. Stir in the cooked rice, warm, then remove from heat and stir in the lime juice and cilantro.

Serves 4

331	Calories
9.7 g	Protein
63.6 g	Carbohydrates
4.5 g	Fat
12%	Calories from Fat
4.8 g	Fiber
16 mg	Sodium
0 mg	Cholesterol

Cooking with Herbs

Pitas with Baba Ghanooj and Mint Couscous

꩜ ꩜

1½ pounds eggplant
⅓ cup lemon juice
⅓ cup tahini
2 cloves garlic, minced
2 tablespoons olive oil
Paprika
2 cups chicken stock
½ cup fresh lemon juice
1½ cups couscous
2 tablespoons fresh
minced mint (or dill
or parsley)
6 Pita bread

PREPARATION TIME:
Less than 1 hour

If you don't want to put this in pita bread, serve it on the side with a meat dish or with vegetables for dipping. The secret to great baba ghanooj is to make sure the eggplant is completely cooked. Couscous and tahini, a sesame seed paste, are found in most markets.

Pierce the eggplant with a fork, place on foil in a 400 degree oven for 40 to 45 minutes, or until very soft. Cool, then peel and remove seeds. Put the eggplant in a food processor and sprinkle with lemon juice. Add tahini and garlic and process until smooth. Spread onto a serving plate and pour a little olive oil over it, then give it a light dusting of paprika.

For the couscous, heat the chicken stock and lemon juice to boiling. Stir in couscous, cover, remove from heat, and set aside for 5 minutes. Stir in the mint. Serve both in pita bread.

Makes enough for 6 to 8 servings

376	Calories
13.4 g	Protein
60.5 g	Carbohydrates
9.5 g	Fat
22%	Calories from Fat
5.7 g	Fiber
302 mg	Sodium
0 mg	Cholesterol

Romesco Salad

୨୰ ❦

1 tomato, peeled, seeded, and chopped

½ red bell pepper, peeled, seeded, and chopped

1 tablespoon red chile pepper flakes

2 cloves garlic, minced

2 tablespoons slivered almonds, toasted

½ cup olive oil

¼ cup white wine vinegar

⅛ teaspoon salt

¼ teaspoon pepper

1 medium zucchini, cut into matchsticks

2 cups green beans, trimmed

½ of a sweet onion, thinly sliced

½ cucumber, seeded and sliced

PREPARATION TIME:
Less than 30 minutes

This Spanish sauce is used on seafood, but I like it on salad. It also works as a sauce for potato salad.

Put the tomato, bell pepper, pepper flakes, garlic, almonds, oil, vinegar, salt, and pepper in blender or food processor and stir until puréed, leaving some texture. Set aside.

Steam or cook the zucchini and green beans until just crisp-tender, then toss with the sweet onion and cucumber slices. Pour romesco sauce over and mix. Serve at room temperature.

Makes 2 servings

639	Calories
7.8 g	Protein
34.1 g	Carbohydrates
56.7 g	Fat
80%	Calories from Fat
8.0 g	Fiber
152 mg	Sodium
0 mg	Cholesterol

GINGER

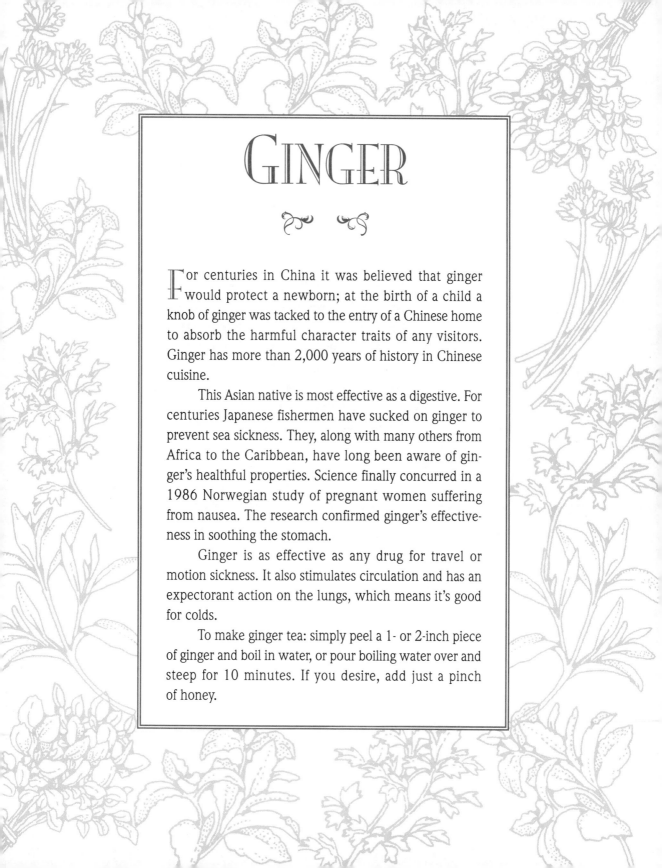

For centuries in China it was believed that ginger would protect a newborn; at the birth of a child a knob of ginger was tacked to the entry of a Chinese home to absorb the harmful character traits of any visitors. Ginger has more than 2,000 years of history in Chinese cuisine.

This Asian native is most effective as a digestive. For centuries Japanese fishermen have sucked on ginger to prevent sea sickness. They, along with many others from Africa to the Caribbean, have long been aware of ginger's healthful properties. Science finally concurred in a 1986 Norwegian study of pregnant women suffering from nausea. The research confirmed ginger's effectiveness in soothing the stomach.

Ginger is as effective as any drug for travel or motion sickness. It also stimulates circulation and has an expectorant action on the lungs, which means it's good for colds.

To make ginger tea: simply peel a 1- or 2-inch piece of ginger and boil in water, or pour boiling water over and steep for 10 minutes. If you desire, add just a pinch of honey.

Although frequently referred to as gingerroot, it is really a rhizome and not a root at all.

I'm hard-pressed to find a lot of things that ginger can't improve. Fresh ginger is a favorite of mine. Among things I add it to:

- Dressings, especially vinaigrettes.
- Grate fresh ginger into drinks, including ginger ale.
- Add to desserts, including whipped cream.
- Good on baked and stewed fruits. Use fresh or crystallized.
- Add to vegetables and any stir-fry.
- Good in many marinades for poultry and fish.
- Stir into puddings.
- Rub on meats before cooking.

Ginger Coconut Rice

2 tablespoons oil or butter
1 tablespoon fresh ginger, peeled and cut into small dice
1¼ cups rice
1½ cups water
½ cup coconut milk

PREPARATION TIME:
Less than 30 minutes
(plus cooking time)

This is an easy variation on everyday rice. I serve it with chicken dishes.

Melt butter and sauté ginger over low heat for 5 minutes. Add rice and stir constantly for 3 to 4 minutes. Add water and coconut milk, then bring to a boil. Reduce heat, cover, and cook 20 minutes, or until liquid is absorbed.

Makes about 2¹/₂ cups (¹/₂ cup per serving)

263	Calories
3.8 g	Protein
37.6 g	Carbohydrates
10.7 g	Fat
36%	Calories from Fat
0.5 g	Fiber
7 mg	Sodium
0 mg	Cholesterol

Fruit with Apple-Peach Sauce

1 tablespoon honey
1 teaspoon sugar
1 cup apple juice
2 tablespoons sliced ginger
3 peaches, peeled, pitted, and sliced
1 nectarine, peeled, pitted, and sliced
 Sliced apples, bananas, grapes, or any fruit

PREPARATION TIME:
Less than 30 minutes (plus chilling time)

This sauce is also good with many dessert breads.

Stir the honey, sugar, and apple juice together in a saucepan. Add ginger, bring to a boil, then simmer for 5 minutes. Add the peach and nectarine and simmer another 5 minutes. Allow to cool slightly, then place in a food processor or blender. Purée, then return to the saucepan and cook another 10 minutes. Remove from heat and refrigerate for at least 30 minutes before serving. Pour over fruit salad.

Makes about 3 cups ($^1/_4$ cup per serving)

33	Calories
0.3 g	Protein
8.1 g	Carbohydrates
0.1 g	Fat
3%	Calories from Fat
0.6 g	Fiber
2 mg	Sodium
0 mg	Cholesterol

Cooking with Herbs

Ginger Muffins

❧ ❧

¼ cup butter
¼ cup sugar
1 egg
½ cup molasses
1½ cups flour
¾ teaspoon baking soda
¼ teaspoon salt
½ teaspoon cinnamon
¼ teaspoon ground cloves
1 teaspoon freshly
    grated ginger
½ cup hot water

PREPARATION TIME:
Less than 30 minutes
(plus baking time)

These muffins are one of the few recipes that can be made with either fresh or ground ginger. If using ground, sift it with the cinnamon and cloves.

Preheat oven to 375 degrees. Cream the butter and sugar together and beat the egg and molasses into the mixture. Sift the flour, baking soda, salt, cinnamon, and ground cloves together (and ground ginger, if using) and stir into the molasses mixture. Stir in ginger, then gradually add the water, beating until smooth. Bake 20 minutes.

Makes 12 muffins

145	Calories
2.2 g	Protein
23.6 g	Carbohydrates
4.6 g	Fat
28%	Calories from Fat
0.5 g	Fiber
172 mg	Sodium
28 mg	Cholesterol

Quick Ginger Aside

1 tablespoon vegetable oil
2 tablespoons fresh grated
   ginger
3 cups peeled, cored, and
   thinly sliced apples
1 cup thinly sliced daikon
2 cups snow peas
2 tablespoons sesame oil

PREPARATION TIME:
Less than 30 minutes

This is an easy side dish that is delicious with many things.

Sauté ginger in vegetable oil over low heat. Add apples, daikon, and snow peas and sauté for another 5 minutes. Remove from heat and toss with sesame oil.

Serves 4

216	Calories
2.5 g	Protein
30.2 g	Carbohydrates
10.9 g	Fat
45%	Calories from Fat
5.0 g	Fiber
9 mg	Sodium
0 mg	Cholesterol

Cooking with Herbs

Curried Pineapple and Ginger Chutney with Rice

❧ ❧

2 cups pineapple, cut
into rings
1 tablespoon vegetable oil
½ sweet onion, diced
1 red or green bell pepper,
diced
1 tablespoon good-quality
curry powder
3 tablespoons fresh
minced ginger (do not
use powdered)
½ cup vinegar
⅓ cup pineapple juice
½ cup brown sugar
1 teaspoon hot pepper
sauce
4 cups cooked rice

PREPARATION TIME:
Less than 30 minutes

I never tire of the combination of pineapple, ginger, and curry flavors. Here's a simple dish that is tangy.

Broil the pineapple rings on an oiled baking sheet until brown (about 4 to 5 minutes each side). Set aside. In a skillet, heat oil and sauté the onion and bell pepper until soft, about 7 minutes. Add remaining ingredients, including the pineapple but not the rice, and bring to a boil. Reduce heat and simmer 10 minutes. Allow to cool for flavors to blend. Serve over rice.

Serves 4 to 6

334	Calories
4.5 g	Protein
72.5 g	Carbohydrates
3.3 g	Fat
9%	Calories from Fat
2.2 g	Fiber
18 mg	Sodium
0 mg	Cholesterol

Blueberry Relish

1 pint blueberries
2 tablespoons lemon juice
2 tablespoons honey
½ teaspoon ground ginger
1 tablespoon chives or
    scallions, minced
Pinch pepper

PREPARATION TIME:
Less than 30 minutes

I have several blueberry bushes in my yard, and they produce too many berries to pick most summers, so we enjoy blueberries in a lot of dishes. Try this relish alongside fish or cold chicken.

Combine all ingredients and chill.

Makes about 2 cups (2 tablespoons per serving)

20	Calories
0.2 g	Protein
5.1 g	Carbohydrates
0.1 g	Fat
3%	Calories from Fat
0.4 g	Fiber
1 mg	Sodium
0 mg	Cholesterol

Cooking with Herbs

Asparagus with Ginger-Lemon Dressing

❧ ❧

1½ teaspoons fresh grated
  ginger
⅛ cup fresh lemon juice
¼ cup olive oil
2 teaspoons walnut oil
1 scallion (white part),
  minced
½ teaspoon fresh minced
  dill, or ¼ teaspoon
  dried
1 pound asparagus,
  steamed or
  microwaved

PREPARATION TIME:
Less than 30 minutes

This light dressing lets the delicate taste of the asparagus come through.

Place ginger and lemon juice in a bowl. Slowly whisk in the olive and walnut oils until emulsified. Stir in scallion and dill, then pour over cooked asparagus.

Serves 4

171	Calories
2.9 g	Protein
6.0 g	Carbohydrates
16.2 g	Fat
85%	Calories from Fat
1.5 g	Fiber
13 mg	Sodium
0 mg	Cholesterol

Ginger Apple Hazelnut Upside-Down Cake

❧ ❧

¼ cup melted butter

⅓ cup brown sugar

2 tablespoons finely chopped crystallized ginger

1 large Granny Smith apple, peeled and thinly sliced

1 tablespoon fresh lemon juice

½ cup flour

½ teaspoon baking powder

¼ teaspoon salt

2 eggs

⅓ cup granulated sugar

1 teaspoon vanilla

¼ cup finely chopped hazelnuts

PREPARATION TIME:
Less than 30 minutes (plus baking time)

This is a delicious twist on the classic cake that usually features pineapple. Serve with whipped cream.

Pour the butter into an 8 × 8 × 2″ baking dish and add brown sugar and ginger. Toss apple slices with lemon juice and arrange them evenly in the bowl. Sift together the flour, baking powder, and salt. Beat the eggs with the granulated sugar and vanilla until thick, about 5 minutes.

Fold the flour mixture into the egg mixture; add hazelnuts and stir gently. Pour over the apple slices and bake 20 to 25 minutes. Run a knife around the edge of the pan and invert the cake onto a serving plate.

Serves 6 to 8

217	Calories
2.8 g	Protein
30.2 g	Carbohydrates
9.9 g	Fat
41%	Calories from Fat
0.8 g	Fiber
168 mg	Sodium
70 mg	Cholesterol

Cooking with Herbs

Chicken with Ginger Barbecue Sauce

୧ ୨

2 medium onions, chopped
5 cloves garlic, chopped
2 tablespoons vegetable oil
1 (2-inch) piece fresh
    ginger, sliced
2 cups tomato sauce
2 tablespoons Dijon
    mustard
1/3 cup vinegar
1 cup water
1 bay leaf
4 tablespoons
    Worcestershire sauce
2 tablespoons brown sugar
2 tablespoons molasses
1/2 teaspoon cayenne
1/4 teaspoon salt
    Boneless, skinless chicken
    breasts or a whole
    tri-tip steak

PREPARATION TIME:
Less than 1 hour

We try to avoid meat, especially red meat, but this is absolutely everything you ever wanted in a barbecue. Use the chicken breasts or a whole chicken, or ask the butcher for an uncut, whole tri-tip steak you can cut yourself after it is cooked. You can use the sauce on rice and vegetables as well.

Sauté onion in oil 3 to 4 minutes; add garlic and sauté until soft, another 3 minutes. Place in a blender or food processor with the ginger and purée. Return to the skillet with remaining ingredients and bring to a boil. Reduce heat and simmer about 25 minutes, stirring occasionally. Barbecue the meat, then serve with the sauce.

Serves 6 to 8 with extra sauce

248	Calories
28.4 g	Protein
16.9 g	Carbohydrates
7.3 g	Fat
26%	Calories from Fat
1.5 g	Fiber
681 mg	Sodium
73 mg	Cholesterol

Gingered Vegetable Stir-Fry

❧ ❧

6 tablespoons rice vinegar
5 tablespoons sugar
¾ cup plus 1½ tablespoons water
2 tablespoons tamari or soy sauce
1 tablespoon cornstarch
1 tablespoon freshly grated ginger
4 tablespoons vegetable oil
1 (2-inch) piece fresh ginger, peeled and cut into small matchsticks
1 red pepper, seeded and julienned
1 onion, halved and thinly sliced
7 to 8 mushrooms, sliced
2 zucchini, sliced
2 cloves garlic, minced
5 to 6 cups of cooked rice

PREPARATION TIME:
Less than 30 minutes

Ginger is so good for the system and absolutely enchants the vegetables in this dish. You can substitute other vegetables for the ones listed here, and add cooked chicken or pork if desired.

Bring vinegar, sugar, and ¾ cup of water to a boil. Reduce heat and simmer 5 minutes. Mix the cornstarch with 1½ tablespoons of water, then stir it into the sauce. Add tamari and cook until thickened, about 5 minutes. Remove from heat and stir in grated ginger.

In a skillet, stir-fry the ginger matchsticks and vegetables until crisp-tender. Cook the pepper and the onion for 2 minutes, then add the garlic, mushrooms, and zucchini for 3 to 4 minutes. Spread the vegetables over the rice; top with the sauce.

Serves 4 to 6

372	Calories
6.4 g	Protein
63.8 g	Carbohydrates
10.1 g	Fat
24%	Calories from Fat
2.0 g	Fiber
356 mg	Sodium
0 mg	Cholesterol

Cooking with Herbs

Warm Gingered Rice Salad

❧ ❧

1 cup rice
2¼ cups vegetable or
　　chicken stock,
　　or water
1 clove garlic, minced
1½ tablespoons minced
　　fresh ginger
3 teaspoons soy sauce
　Juice of 1 lemon
1 teaspoon lemon zest
¼ cup olive oil
3 green onions, chopped
1 red pepper, roasted if
　　desired, and chopped

PREPARATION TIME:
Less than 30 minutes

This recipe was inspired by a salad idea I saw from the late Bert Greene.

Boil the stock and add the rice, cover, and cook 17 minutes over low heat. Combine the remaining ingredients, except the onions and pepper, and whisk together well. Stir into rice, then mix in green onion and pepper.

Serves 4

309	Calories
4.2 g	Protein
41.7 g	Carbohydrates
14.0 g	Fat
40%	Calories from Fat
0.8 g	Fiber
333 mg	Sodium
0 mg	Cholesterol

Pineapple-Kiwi Smoothie

3 kiwis, peeled
⅓ cup pineapple juice
1 teaspoon freshly grated
   ginger
⅔ cup ice

PREPARATION TIME:
Less than 30 minutes

Refreshing and healthful, this is a smoothie to delight kids and adults.

Place in a blender and purée.

Makes 2 servings

94	Calories
1.3 g	Protein
23.2 g	Carbohydrates
0.6 g	Fat
5%	Calories from Fat
3.9 g	Fiber
8 mg	Sodium
0 mg	Cholesterol

Lemon Verbena

Lemon verbena comes to us from South America, but it has been grown in Europe since the 18th century, and is also cultivated in Asia and Africa. Both the leaves and flowers may be used in cooking.

South Americans have used the herb in soaps and cosmetics, and in drinks as a mild medicinal herbal. Herbalists today suggest it be used for nausea, dyspepsia, and flatulence. While difficult to find fresh, you may find dried lemon verbena at herb shops.

If you are unable to find lemon verbena, but want to make these recipes, substitute lemon zest, using just a little less than the verbena called for here.

Here are ideas for using the herb:

- Add to teas and drinks, including lemonade.
- Substitute for lemon zest in cooked foods.
- Make a tea by infusing the leaves with boiling water for a few minutes. Add a touch of honey if desired.
- Add to fruit salads.
- Stir into cream salad dressings.

Lemon Bread with Lemon Sauce

❧ ❧

Bread

1/2 cup vegetable shortening

3/4 cup sugar

2 eggs

1 1/4 cups flour

1 teaspoon baking powder

1/4 teaspoon salt

1/2 cup milk

1 1/2 tablespoons finely chopped lemon verbena

1 tablespoon lemon juice

Sauce

1/2 cup sugar

1 tablespoon cornstarch

1 cup boiling water

1 1/4 tablespoons butter

1 teaspoon minced lemon verbena

3 tablespoons lemon juice

PREPARATION TIME:
Less than 30 minutes
(plus baking time)

This lemon bread is also good with whipped cream or fresh fruit. If you don't have verbena you may substitute lemon zest.

Preheat oven to 350 degrees. Grease and flour an 8 1/2-inch loaf pan. Combine the shortening and sugar and beat well to blend. Add eggs, beating the first well into the mixture before adding the second. In a separate bowl, combine flour with baking powder and salt and mix well. Add this to the shortening mix, along with the milk, lemon verbena, and lemon juice, and beat until smooth. Spread the mixture evenly in the pan and bake about 1 hour, or until a toothpick inserted into the middle comes out clean.

To make the sauce, combine sugar and cornstarch in a pot over medium heat, and gradually add boiling water. Cook 7 minutes, stirring, until thickened. Remove from heat and stir in remaining ingredients. Spoon sauce over sliced bread.

Makes one loaf (16 slices)

174	Calories
2.1 g	Protein
23.8 g	Carbohydrates
8.3 g	Fat
42%	Calories from Fat
0.3 g	Fiber
75 mg	Sodium
31 mg	Cholesterol

Cooking with Herbs

Lemon Verbena Ice Cream

4 cups milk
½ cup sugar
⅓ cup honey
4 to 5 fresh whole lemon
    verbena leaves, bruised

PREPARATION TIME:
More than 1 hour

This is a delightful ice cream. You might try mint leaves if lemon verbena leaves aren't available.

Warm milk until hot, but do not boil. Remove from heat and stir in remaining ingredients. Cover and let sit until it has reached room temperature, about an hour. Strain and discard leaves. Freeze in an ice cream freezer according to manufacturer's directions. Freeze for 4 hours before serving.

Makes about 4 cups (¹/₂ cup per serving)

149 Calories
4.1 g Protein
29.1 g Carbohydrates
2.3 g Fat
14% Calories from Fat
0.0 g Fiber
62 mg Sodium
9 mg Cholesterol

MARJORAM

This Mediterranean native, a close relative to oregano, was thought to keep milk fresh during the Middle Ages. It was also used as an anti-depressant. Sweet marjoram is what is most commonly found in the United States. Wild marjoram is commonly called oregano.

Marjoram is used little by herbalists for medicinal purposes, although this herb of the mint family is thought of as an aid to digestion.

However, marjoram does enjoy very wide use as a culinary herb:

- Add to soups, especially spinach soup.
- Rub on meats before roasting.
- Add to stuffings.
- Stir into omelets and other egg dishes.
- Sprinkle over sautéed mushrooms.
- Use in fish sauces and with baked, broiled, or grilled fish.
- Use with vegetables, especially zucchini and carrots.
- Use as a substitute for sage in some recipes.
- Add to meat and vegetable stews.
- Good with chicken and other poultry dishes. Rub a chicken with marjoram before roasting.
- Use a pinch in sauces.
- Add to vinaigrettes and other dressings.

Zucchini and Corn with Herbs

❧ ❧

2 tablespoons vegetable
  oil
2 small zucchini, sliced
½ sweet onion, halved and
  thinly sliced
1½ cups sweet corn, cooked
1 small sweet red or green
  pepper, cut into strips
2 teaspoons fresh, finely
  chopped marjoram
1 tablespoon fresh, finely
  chopped basil
2 teaspoons balsamic
  vinegar

PREPARATION TIME:
Less than 30 minutes

This is best with fresh herbs, but you can substitute dried marjoram if you must. A nice and easy side dish.

Sauté the zucchini, onion, corn, and pepper in a skillet with oil over low-medium heat for 6 minutes. Add the fresh herbs, mix well, and sauté another minute; add vinegar and cook another 2 minutes. Serve over rice, if desired.

Serves 4 to 6

87	Calories
1.7 g	Protein
10.9 g	Carbohydrates
4.9 g	Fat
50%	Calories from Fat
1.6 g	Fiber
3 mg	Sodium
0 mg	Cholesterol

Cooking with Herbs

Corn Chowder

❧ ❧

4 tablespoons vegetable oil
1 onion, minced
½ cup flour
3 cups vegetable stock
¼ cup dry white wine
½ red bell pepper, minced
2 cups cream
1 teaspoon chopped fresh
    marjoram, or
    ½ teaspoon dried
3 cups fresh corn kernels,
    or frozen and defrosted
3 tablespoons fresh chopped
    cilantro or parsley
1 cup grated jack cheese

PREPARATION TIME:
Less than 30 minutes

This soup is best with fresh corn, of course, and makes a warming fall dish.

Sauté onion in oil until soft, about 5 minutes. Add flour and stir for about 3 minutes. Add stock and wine and continue stirring until thickened slightly. Add remaining ingredients (except cheese), bring to a boil, and simmer 10 to 12 minutes. Remove to a blender or food processor and chop but don't completely purée, then return to the saucepan and stir in the cheese.

Serves 4 to 6

378	Calories
10.9 g	Protein
30.3 g	Carbohydrates
24.9 g	Fat
59%	Calories from Fat
2.4 g	Fiber
142 mg	Sodium
46 mg	Cholesterol

Herb and Potato Ravioli

෪ ᰨ

2 tablespoons extra-virgin
   olive oil
1 onion, finely chopped
3 potatoes, peeled and cut
   crosswise into
   $\frac{1}{8}$-inch slices
1$\frac{1}{2}$ tablespoons fresh
   minced marjoram, or
   1 teaspoon dried
1 tablespoon fresh minced
   rosemary, or
   1 teaspoon dried
2$\frac{1}{3}$ cups flour
3 large eggs plus
   2 egg yolks
$\frac{1}{4}$ cup marscarpone or
   light cream cheese
$\frac{1}{2}$ cup ricotta cheese

PREPARATION TIME:
A little over 1 hour

404 Calories
13.1 g Protein
54.3 g Carbohydrates
14.6 g Fat
32% Calories from Fat
2.6 g Fiber
69 mg Sodium
197 mg Cholesterol

If you want to make these quickly, pick up some won ton wrappers and use them as you would the ravioli dough. These are good drizzled with olive oil, butter, or with a tomato-based sauce.

Over medium heat, add oil to a skillet and sauté onion until soft, about 5 minutes. Add the potatoes and cook until tender, about 15 minutes. Add marjoram and rosemary and cook another 2 minutes. Remove from heat.

While the mixture cools, make the pasta dough. Make a well in the center of the flour and break the 3 eggs into it. Lightly beat the eggs, then gradually incorporate the flour into the eggs. Knead the dough until it is smooth and not too soft, about 5 minutes. Roll out the pasta on a dusted board. Flatten the dough and roll out evenly. Sprinkle with flour and cover with a towel for 10 minutes, until it is dry.

In a mixing bowl, combine the marscarpone, ricotta, and the room temperature potato mixture. Mash together, then add the egg yolks and stir until smooth.

Cut the pasta into strips about 4 inches wide and 10 or 11 inches long. On half the strips place a little of the potato mixture. Cover with an unfilled strip, brush the edges with cold water, and seal. Cut into squares and use remaining dough to make more ravioli.

Bring 5 quarts of water to a boil. Add the ravioli and cook until they rise to the surface, about 2 minutes. Top with melted butter, olive oil, or a favorite sauce.

Serves 4 to 6

Cooking with Herbs

Lasagna

꥟ ꥞

1 tablespoon olive oil
½ onion, finely chopped
2 cloves garlic, minced
6 tomatoes, chopped
1 tablespoon fresh
   marjoram, or
   1 teaspoon dried
   Pinch fresh dill
2 tablespoons fresh minced
   basil, or 2 teaspoons
   dried
¼ teaspoon pepper
½ pound lasagna noodles,
   cooked
16 ounces ricotta cheese
2 cups grated mozzarella
½ cup grated Parmesan
   cheese
1 zucchini, diced
5 to 6 mushrooms, sliced
   and then halved
3 cups fresh chopped
   spinach

PREPARATION TIME:
Less than 30 minutes
(plus baking time)

This is an easy lasagna to make, and a healthful one. A little dill gives it a sweeter flavor.

Preheat oven to 350 degrees. Heat oil in a saucepan and sauté onion and garlic for 5 minutes. Purée the tomatoes, then add onion and garlic, along with the marjoram, dill, basil, and pepper. Simmer 15 minutes, remove from heat, and place enough sauce to cover the bottom of a 13 × 9″ baking dish. Place a layer of pasta, then top with one third of the remaining ingredients, including sauce. Repeat for two more layers. Bake until hot, about 40 minutes.

Serves 4 to 6

436	Calories
28.1 g	Protein
42.6 g	Carbohydrates
17.7 g	Fat
36%	Calories from Fat
4.1 g	Fiber
429 mg	Sodium
49 mg	Cholesterol

Herb and Cheese-filled Zucchini

6 medium zucchini
3 tablespoons olive oil
3 cloves garlic, minced
¼ cup chopped shallots
½ teaspoon fresh marjoram,
    or ¼ teaspoon dried
½ teaspoon fresh thyme,
    or ¼ teaspoon dried
⅓ cup white wine
½ cup bread crumbs
¾ cup grated Parmesan
    cheese

PREPARATION TIME:
Less than 30 minutes
(plus baking time)

I have tried a variety of combinations for zucchini, which I've offered in other books. I came up with this one when I had an abundance of late summer squash.

Preheat oven to 350 degrees. Steam the zucchini whole for 5 minutes, until just softened. Trim the ends and cut in half lengthwise. Scoop out the center, making a hollow for the stuffing.

Sauté the garlic, shallots, and herbs in oil over medium-low heat for about 10 minutes. Add white wine, increase heat to high, and cook for about 4 minutes, or until the wine is reduced by half. Remove the garlic mixture to a separate bowl and combine with the bread crumbs and ½ cup of the Parmesan. Place the mixture into the zucchini and then top with the remaining Parmesan. Bake in an oiled baking dish for 25 minutes, until brown.

Serves 6

165	Calories
6.9 g	Protein
11.7 g	Carbohydrates
10.3 g	Fat
56%	Calories from Fat
1.8 g	Fiber
250 mg	Sodium
8 mg	Cholesterol

Cooking with Herbs

MINT

Mint, which comes from the Mediterranean areas of Europe, was thought in ancient times to stimulate thinking and was given to scholars. It has a long history of culinary use as well, with mint sauce recipes dating from the third century.

In the Middle Ages, mint was thought to help headaches, digestive problems—even bee stings. Today herbalists use mint for indigestion, colds, and as an anti-parasitic. It has been shown effective for colic, although you should never use it as an inhalant for babies. Mint also helps stimulate the gall bladder and liver, and it contains oils which may help heal ulcers. Mint is used in pain-relieving oils and liniments and helps increase blood flow to any area where it is applied.

Mint's aromatic flavor is good in a variety of dishes:

- Add mint leaves to dressings, especially creamy and vegetable dressings.
- Use a sprig in iced beverages.
- Sprinkle fresh mint leaves over fruit salads.
- Add to sauces, especially those for lamb.
- Cook with vegetables, such as carrots, peas, and zucchini.
- Mix into syrups.
- Use in fish sauces, and add to fish when cooked.
- Mix into ice cream, gelatins, frostings.
- Stir into soup, especially split pea or cream soups.

Mint Tea

1 bunch fresh mint, rinsed
  and trimmed
2 tablespoons sugar
4 cups boiling water

PREPARATION TIME:
Less than 30 minutes

Quick and refreshing. Grow mint in your garden, and you won't need teabags.

Place the mint and sugar in a saucepan, add boiling water, stir, cover, and steep 5 minutes.

Serves 4

24	Calories
0.1 g	Protein
6.3 g	Carbohydrates
0.0 g	Fat
0%	Calories from Fat
0.0 g	Fiber
3 mg	Sodium
0 mg	Cholesterol

Cooking with Herbs

Split Pea Soup with Mint

༂ ༂

2 cups split peas, soaked in
    cold water overnight,
    and drained
1 large onion, chopped
1 carrot, chopped
1 teaspoon fresh thyme, or
    $1/2$ teaspoon dried
1 tablespoon chopped mint
    leaves
1 teaspoon salt
    Pepper

PREPARATION TIME:
Less than 30 minutes
(plus simmer time)

I used to avoid adding mint to my recipes, fearing that it would overpower foods. I've gradually learned to use the power of this herb to enhance flavors, as it does in this soup.

Place split peas in a pot with $4^{1}/_{2}$ cups of cold water and bring to a boil. Add the onion and carrot and cover. Simmer over low heat for 2 hours, adding water if it becomes too thick. Add thyme, mint, salt, and pepper, and purée in batches. Return to the pot to heat.

Serves 4 to 6

262	Calories
17.0 g	Protein
48.6 g	Carbohydrates
0.9 g	Fat
3%	Calories from Fat
5.1 g	Fiber
418 mg	Sodium
0 mg	Cholesterol

Mulligatawny with Cucumber–Mint Raita

❧ ❧

Raita

1 cucumber, peeled,
    seeded, and coarsely
    grated
3 cups yogurt
1/2 teaspoon ground cumin
1 teaspoon salt
4 mint leaves, finely
    chopped

Soup

2 tablespoons vegetable
    oil
2 tablespoons butter
1 onion, chopped
1 clove garlic, minced
2 tablespoons fresh ginger
1 1/2 tablespoons curry
    powder
6 cups chicken stock
2 tomatoes, peeled,
    seeded, and finely
    chopped
1 tart apple, cored,
    peeled, and finely
    chopped
1 stalk celery, sliced

PREPARATION TIME:
More than 1 hour

The delicious spiciness of this traditional Indian soup is offset by the cool mint and cucumber flavors.

Combine the cucumber, yogurt, cumin, salt, and mint leaves. Chill. Heat the oil and melt the butter in a pot, then add onion, garlic, and ginger and sauté 3 to 4 minutes. Stir in curry and mix well. Add stock, tomatoes, apple, and celery and bring to a boil. Cover and simmer 30 minutes. Serve with a dollop of the cucumber-mint raita in each bowl.

Serves 6 to 8

150	Calories
7.5 g	Protein
15.3 g	Carbohydrates
7.1 g	Fat
43%	Calories from Fat
1.5 g	Fiber
439 mg	Sodium
10 mg	Cholesterol

Cooking with Herbs

Raspberry Mint Seltzer

20 raspberries
20 mint leaves
 4 teaspoons lemon juice
 1 teaspoon sugar (optional)
   Seltzer

PREPARATION TIME:
Less than 30 minutes

Here's a summer Saturday brightener. Quick and very refreshing.

Alternate 5 raspberries and 5 mint leaves on toothpicks or skewers. Fill four 12-ounce glasses with 1 teaspoon each of lemon juice and $1/4$ teaspoon of sugar. Fill with seltzer and stir. Place the toothpicks in the seltzer and let sit for 5 minutes before serving.

Makes 4 glasses

6	Calories
0.0 g	Protein
1.8 g	Carbohydrates
0.0 g	Fat
0%	Calories from Fat
0.0 g	Fiber
50 mg	Sodium
0 mg	Cholesterol

Mint and Apple Chutney

੭੭ ੶੶

1 Granny Smith or other
  firm apple
$\frac{1}{2}$ orange
$\frac{1}{2}$ lemon, peeled
$\frac{1}{2}$ cup currants
$\frac{1}{2}$ cup fresh mint
  Dash hot pepper sauce,
  or to taste

PREPARATION TIME:
Less than 30 minutes

I serve this chutney with lamb dishes or alongside spicy Indian or Mexican foods.

Peel and core the apple, peel the orange, and cut into pieces. Place all ingredients in a food processor and chop, adding a little water to blend. Do not purée.

Makes about 2 cups (1 tablespoon per serving)

13 Calories
0.2 g Protein
3.5 g Carbohydrates
0.0 g Fat
0% Calories from Fat
0.5 g Fiber
1 mg Sodium
0 mg Cholesterol

Cooking with Herbs

Salad with Peas, Walnuts, and Mint

∾ ∾

4 cups mesclun or salad greens
1 sweet onion, thinly sliced
$\frac{1}{2}$ cup chopped walnuts
1 tablespoon fresh chopped mint leaves
1 cup fresh peas, cooked and cooled
2 teaspoons lemon juice
1 tablespoon olive oil

PREPARATION TIME:
Less than 30 minutes

This was one of the first things I created with mint, and it remains a favorite. I fix it frequently in the summer.

Wash and dry the salad greens. Set aside. Combine the onion, nuts, mint, and peas in a bowl and mix well. Combine the lemon juice and olive oil, toss with the onion mixture, then combine with the greens.

Serves 4 to 6

91	Calories
2.9 g	Protein
8.4 g	Carbohydrates
5.7 g	Fat
56%	Calories from Fat
1.5 g	Fiber
6 mg	Sodium
0 mg	Cholesterol

Mahi–Mahi with Fruit Salsa

ᗧ᙮ ᙮ᗧ

½ pint strawberries,
    quartered
½ papaya, peeled, seeded,
    and diced
½ mango, peeled
    and diced
1½ teaspoons lime juice
1½ teaspoons sugar
¼ serrano, seeded and
    minced
1½ teaspoons minced
    epazote or mint
2 pounds mahi-mahi or
    other fish

PREPARATION TIME:
Less than 30 minutes

My good friend John Lien likes mahi-mahi with this salsa, but you could try red snapper, bluefish, or another fish of your choice.

Combine all except fish in a bowl and stir. Let stand 10 minutes. Grill or broil fish for 2 or 3 minutes per side. Spoon salsa over each serving.

Makes about 2 cups of salsa (serves 4)

241	Calories
41.6 g	Protein
13.2 g	Carbohydrates
1.8 g	Fat
7%	Calories from Fat
2.1 g	Fiber
198 mg	Sodium
162 mg	Cholesterol

Mint-Mango Chutney

1 large mango, peeled and diced

½ cup fresh chopped mint leaves

3 tablespoons lime juice

2 tablespoons orange juice

2 tablespoons fresh grated ginger

1 teaspoon jalapeño, seeded and minced

PREPARATION TIME:
Less than 30 minutes

This goes nicely with grilled tuna, or try it with rice.

Combine all ingredients and mix well.

Makes about 2 cups (1 tablespoon per serving)

9	Calories
0.1 g	Protein
2.3 g	Carbohydrates
0.0 g	Fat
0%	Calories from Fat
0.3 g	Fiber
1 mg	Sodium
0 mg	Cholesterol

Grilled Pompano with Mint Pesto

1 cup (packed) fresh mint
    leaves
$\frac{1}{2}$ cup fresh Italian parsley
1 large clove garlic
$\frac{1}{2}$ cup chopped walnuts or
    pine nuts
$\frac{1}{2}$ cup extra-virgin olive oil
$\frac{1}{8}$ teaspoon salt
$\frac{1}{8}$ teaspoon pepper
1 pound pompano (sunfish)

PREPARATION TIME:
Less than 30 minutes

This pesto is also good with red snapper and is a perfect complement to lamb.

Blend all except fish in a food processor or blender until smooth, keeping a little bit of texture. Grill fish about 5 minutes per side, then serve with pesto on the side.

Serves 4

477	Calories
22.1 g	Protein
3.2 g	Carbohydrates
42.3 g	Fat
80%	Calories from Fat
1.1 g	Fiber
144 mg	Sodium
55 mg	Cholesterol

Cooking with Herbs

Broiled Cod with Cucumber–Mint Sauce

1 cucumber, peeled,
    seeded, and chopped
Zest of 1 lemon
5 to 6 fresh mint leaves
Juice of ½ lemon
¼ teaspoon white pepper
½ teaspoon honey
⅛ to ¼ cup white vinegar
1 teaspoon salt
¾ cup peanut or walnut oil
1 pound cod fillets or other
    white fish

PREPARATION TIME:
Less than 30 minutes

Make this cool and refreshing sauce with fresh, never dried, mint. It's also good with spicy food, especially curried meats.

Preheat the broiler. Blend the cucumber, lemon zest, and mint in a processor until smooth. Add the lemon juice, pepper, honey, vinegar, and salt and blend briefly, then pour in the oil in a steady stream with the machine running. Brush the cod with olive oil and place in the oven, about 4 to 5 inches from the source of the heat. Change pan position and baste frequently, cooking about 10 minutes for each inch of thickness. Drizzle sauce over fish.

Serves 4

458	Calories
19.0 g	Protein
4.6 g	Carbohydrates
41.3 g	Fat
81%	Calories from Fat
0.8 g	Fiber
597 mg	Sodium
45 mg	Cholesterol

Black Bean and Mint Salad

❧ ❧

3 cups cooked black beans, rinsed

1 ½ cups sweet onion, finely chopped

½ cup crumbled feta cheese

⅓ cup fresh mint, tightly packed, finely chopped

3 tablespoons fresh lime juice

2 tablespoons extra-virgin olive oil

Salt and pepper

PREPARATION TIME:
Less than 30 minutes

This is a salad to surprise guests. Its color and flavor complement fish dishes and barbecues.

Mix all ingredients well. Serve at room temperature.

Serves 4 to 6

196	Calories
9.5 g	Protein
25.2 g	Carbohydrates
7.0 g	Fat
32%	Calories from Fat
4.3 g	Fiber
107 mg	Sodium
8 mg	Cholesterol

Cooking with Herbs

MUSTARD

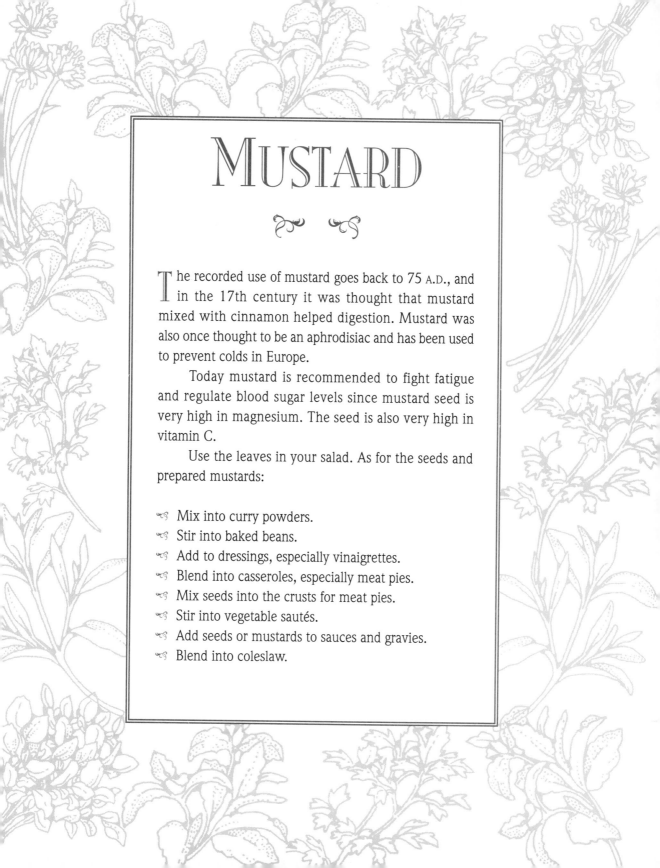

The recorded use of mustard goes back to 75 A.D., and in the 17th century it was thought that mustard mixed with cinnamon helped digestion. Mustard was also once thought to be an aphrodisiac and has been used to prevent colds in Europe.

Today mustard is recommended to fight fatigue and regulate blood sugar levels since mustard seed is very high in magnesium. The seed is also very high in vitamin C.

Use the leaves in your salad. As for the seeds and prepared mustards:

- Mix into curry powders.
- Stir into baked beans.
- Add to dressings, especially vinaigrettes.
- Blend into casseroles, especially meat pies.
- Mix seeds into the crusts for meat pies.
- Stir into vegetable sautés.
- Add seeds or mustards to sauces and gravies.
- Blend into coleslaw.

Mediterranean Salad

6 cups mesclun or mixed
greens
2 cups cauliflower florets
½ sweet red pepper, cut into
matchsticks
½ cup thinly sliced
red onion
¼ cup pitted and sliced
black olives
¾ cup extra-virgin olive oil
4 tablespoons balsamic
vinegar
½ teaspoon dry mustard
1 clove garlic, minced
¼ teaspoon pepper
1 tablespoon minced
parsley

PREPARATION TIME:
Less than 30 minutes

*Enjoy this easy salad at lunch. Add other vegetables or croutons
to the salad if desired.*

Combine the vegetables in a bowl. Whisk together remaining
ingredients and toss with salad.

Serves 4

423	Calories
2.6 g	Protein
12.3 g	Carbohydrates
42.0 g	Fat
89%	Calories from Fat
2.6 g	Fiber
104 mg	Sodium
0 mg	Cholesterol

Pumpkin Soup

3½ cups pumpkin purée
2 teaspoons dry mustard
2 tablespoons butter
2½ tablespoons curry powder
1½ tablespoons fresh grated ginger
1 teaspoon allspice
6 cups chicken broth
1 cup coconut milk, or ¾ cup yogurt
½ cup yogurt
½ cup cashews (optional)

PREPARATION TIME:
Less than 30 minutes
(plus simmer time)

I created this soup one fall as my contribution to a holiday dinner. I use my own special curry blend; be sure to use a good-quality, mild curry powder, nothing too hot and spicy.

Stir the mustard into the pumpkin. Melt butter in a saucepan; add curry powder, ginger, and allspice. Stir in the broth and pumpkin purée. Simmer 40 minutes. Stir in the milk, yogurt, and cashews, if desired.

Serves 6 to 8

152	Calories
4.7 g	Protein
13.9 g	Carbohydrates
10.1 g	Fat
60%	Calories from Fat
2.1 g	Fiber
118 mg	Sodium
8 mg	Cholesterol

Mustard

Halibut in Mustard Sauce

¾ cup water
⅛ cup white vinegar
1 tablespoon butter
1 tablespoon flour
½ teaspoon salt
1 tablespoon Dijon
mustard
1½ pounds halibut

PREPARATION TIME:
Less than 30 minutes

I grew up catching halibut in California, and it has always been one of my favorite fish. Now I buy it fresh whenever I can on the Oregon coast.

Combine water and vinegar. Set aside. Melt butter in a saucepan and stir in the flour, stirring constantly until the mixture turns brown, about 5 minutes. Add water mixture and stir until free of lumps and thickened, another 5 minutes. Remove from heat and stir in the mustard. Grill or poach the fish and serve with sauce.

Serves 4

215	Calories
33.6 g	Protein
2.2 g	Carbohydrates
7.2 g	Fat
30%	Calories from Fat
0.1 g	Fiber
484 mg	Sodium
59 mg	Cholesterol

Cooking with Herbs

Oregano

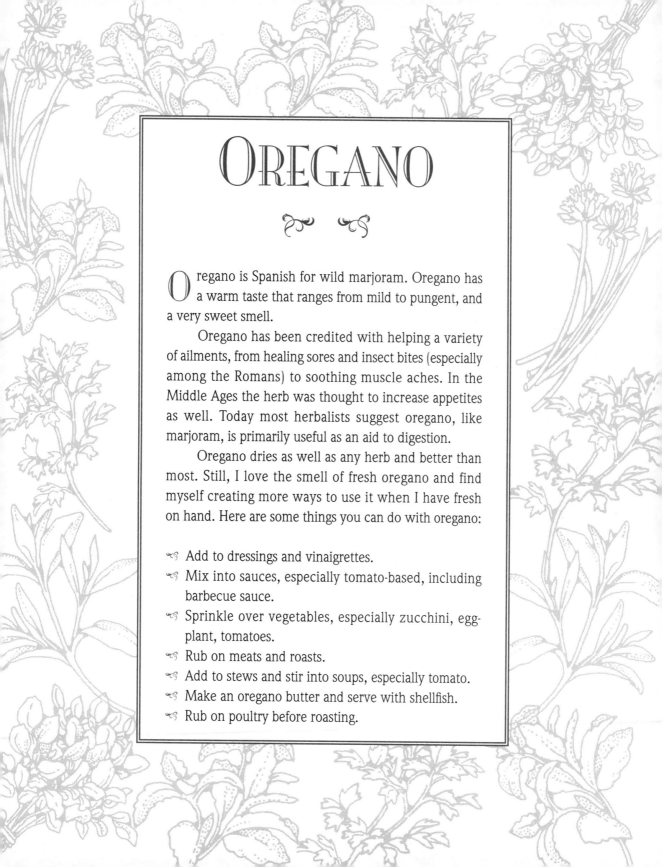

O regano is Spanish for wild marjoram. Oregano has a warm taste that ranges from mild to pungent, and a very sweet smell.

Oregano has been credited with helping a variety of ailments, from healing sores and insect bites (especially among the Romans) to soothing muscle aches. In the Middle Ages the herb was thought to increase appetites as well. Today most herbalists suggest oregano, like marjoram, is primarily useful as an aid to digestion.

Oregano dries as well as any herb and better than most. Still, I love the smell of fresh oregano and find myself creating more ways to use it when I have fresh on hand. Here are some things you can do with oregano:

- Add to dressings and vinaigrettes.
- Mix into sauces, especially tomato-based, including barbecue sauce.
- Sprinkle over vegetables, especially zucchini, eggplant, tomatoes.
- Rub on meats and roasts.
- Add to stews and stir into soups, especially tomato.
- Make an oregano butter and serve with shellfish.
- Rub on poultry before roasting.

Greek Lemon Chicken

❧ ❧

¾ cup lemon juice
⅓ cup extra-virgin olive oil
3 cloves garlic, minced
3 tablespoons lemon zest
1½ tablespoons fresh
   chopped oregano, or
   2 teaspoons dried
3 tablespoons chopped
   parsley
1 chicken, cut into pieces

PREPARATION TIME:
Less than 30 minutes
(plus marinating time)

The flavors here are a Mediterranean treat. Serve with rice or rice pilaf.

Combine all ingredients except chicken. Mix well, then brush on chicken pieces and let marinate for about an hour before grilling.

Serves 4 to 6

353	Calories
27.3 g	Protein
3.8 g	Carbohydrates
25.5 g	Fat
65%	Calories from Fat
0.1 g	Fiber
82 mg	Sodium
87 mg	Cholesterol

Cooking with Herbs

Chicken with Feta

 

²⁄₃ pound feta cheese, diced
2 tablespoons fresh minced
    oregano, or 2
    teaspoons dried
2 cloves garlic, minced
¹⁄₃ cup lemon juice
1 large chicken
¹⁄₂ cup extra-virgin olive oil
1 teaspoon fresh thyme,
    or ¹⁄₂ teaspoon dried
¹⁄₄ teaspoon salt
¹⁄₄ teaspoon pepper

PREPARATION TIME:
Less than 30 minutes
(plus roasting time)

This is a rich, delicious change from any chicken you've tasted. Of course, this is from someone who loves feta cheese.

Preheat oven to 450 degrees. Combine the cheese, oregano, garlic, and 2 tablespoons of the lemon juice. Stuff this mixture into the cavity of the chicken and skewer closed.

    Mix remaining lemon juice with the olive oil, thyme, salt, and pepper, then rub on the outside of the chicken. Bake about 55 minutes.

Serves 4 to 6

585	Calories
40.1 g	Protein
3.8 g	Carbohydrates
45.1 g	Fat
69%	Calories from Fat
0.0 g	Fiber
756 mg	Sodium
150 mg	Cholesterol

Simple Black Bean Chili with Orange Jicama Salsa

❧ ❧

Chili

1 tablespoon olive oil
1 onion, chopped
2 cloves garlic, minced
½ bell pepper, diced
1 tablespoon dried oregano
1 tablespoon chili powder
2 (16-ounce) cans crushed
   tomatoes
4 cups chicken stock
   or water
6 cups cooked or canned
   black beans, rinsed and
   drained

Salsa

2 navel oranges, peeled and
   sectioned, with juice
2 green onions, sliced
1 tablespoon lemon zest
1 (1-pound) jicama, peeled
   and cut into
   matchsticks
2 tablespoons extra-virgin
   olive oil
⅛ teaspoon cumin
⅛ teaspoon ground
   coriander

PREPARATION TIME:
Less than 30 minutes
(plus simmer time)

This chili is a snap to make. You can cut the amount of liquid if you like and serve it in tortillas with the salsa, or serve the salsa in the chili or on the side.

Pour the oil into a pot and add onion, garlic, pepper, and spices. Cook until the vegetables are soft, about 8 minutes. Add tomatoes, stock, and beans and bring to a boil. Reduce heat and cook over low heat, partially covered, for 2 hours.

While the chili cooks, combine the remaining ingredients well, cover, and place in the refrigerator to chill. Add a spoonful of the salsa to each serving of chili.

Serves 6 to 8

285	Calories
14.9 g	Protein
49.0 g	Carbohydrates
4.6 g	Fat
15%	Calories from Fat
7.9 g	Fiber
355 mg	Sodium
0 mg	Cholesterol

Cooking with Herbs

Roasted Red Pepper Pizza

❧ ❧

1 ready-to-bake pizza crust
    or focaccia bread
4 tablespoons extra-virgin
    olive oil, plus extra for
    rubbing on bread
2 red peppers, roasted and
    julienned
3 cloves garlic, minced
1/3 cup dry red wine
10 to 12 olives, pitted
    and sliced
1/8 teaspoon salt
1/8 teaspoon pepper
1 tablespoon fresh oregano,
    or 1 teaspoon dried
1 cup grated mozzarella
    cheese

PREPARATION TIME:
Less than 30 minutes

Use the pizza crust described in Basic Recipes, or try this with focaccia bread.

Preheat oven to 450 degrees. Rub the bread or crust with a little olive oil. Heat half the remaining olive oil and sauté the peppers and garlic over medium-low heat, about 8 minutes. Add wine, olives, salt, pepper, and, if using dried add the oregano; cook 3 to 4 minutes. Spread the filling over the bread and sprinkle with fresh oregano and cheese. Drizzle the remaining olive oil on top. Bake about 15 minutes.

Serves 4

403	Calories
13.5 g	Protein
35.9 g	Carbohydrates
21.3 g	Fat
48%	Calories from Fat
2.0 g	Fiber
775 mg	Sodium
16 mg	Cholesterol

Greek Salad

༨ ༩

Dressing

8 tablespoons extra-virgin
  olive oil

3 tablespoons fresh lemon
  juice

2 tablespoons red wine
  vinegar

1 clove garlic, crushed

1 tablespoon fresh oregano,
  or scant 1 teaspoon
  dried

½ teaspoon salt

½ teaspoon pepper

Salad

2 to 3 large ripe tomatoes,
  cut into chunks

1 Vidalia, Walla Walla, or
  red onion, halved and
  thinly sliced

1 cucumber, peeled,
  seeded, and sliced

1 sweet red pepper, seeded
  and cut into chunks

⅓ cup calamata olives,
  pitted and halved

¾ cup feta cheese, cut into
  large dice

PREPARATION TIME:
Less than 30 minutes

Simple things are often the best. If you've never made a Greek salad with fresh oregano, you're in for a wonderful summer treat.

Combine the dressing ingredients (first seven) in a small bowl and whisk well to blend. Discard the garlic. Toss the tomatoes, onion, cucumber, red pepper, and olives in a large bowl and top with chunks of feta. Toss with dressing and serve.

Serves 4 to 6

247	Calories
3.2 g	Protein
8.3 g	Carbohydrates
23.5 g	Fat
85%	Calories from Fat
1.6 g	Fiber
542 mg	Sodium
13 mg	Cholesterol

Cooking with Herbs

Chicken with Mushrooms and Herbs

❧ ❧

¼ cup butter, softened
2 chicken breasts, boned and split into halves
½ pound mushrooms, thinly sliced
1 teaspoon fresh chopped oregano, or ½ teaspoon dried
1 teaspoon fresh chopped basil, or ½ teaspoon dried
2 shallots, finely chopped
⅛ cup dry white wine
⅛ cup extra-virgin olive oil
3 tablespoons lemon juice

PREPARATION TIME:
Less than 1 hour
(plus marinating time)

This dish has a wonderful aroma while cooking. Cook some rice and stir a little dill into it as a side dish.

Spread the butter on the bottom of a baking dish. Place the chicken in a single layer on top and sprinkle with mushrooms. Combine the remaining ingredients in a bowl and pour over the chicken. Cover and refrigerate for 6 hours or more. Preheat oven to 350 degrees, remove cover, and bake 40 minutes.

Serves 4 to 6

387	Calories
30.8 g	Protein
5.4 g	Carbohydrates
26.8 g	Fat
63%	Calories from Fat
0.9 g	Fiber
195 mg	Sodium
116 mg	Cholesterol

Pepper and Rice Casserole

༜ ༜

1 tablespoon butter or
   olive oil
1 onion, chopped
1 sweet red pepper,
   seeded and minced
2 cloves garlic, minced
2½ cups cooked rice
2 zucchini, shredded
2 tomatoes, peeled and
   chopped
¼ cup freshly grated
   Parmesan cheese
   Dash Tabasco or other
   hot pepper sauce
2 tablespoons vegetable
   broth or water
2 teaspoons fresh chopped
   oregano, or
   1 teaspoon dried

PREPARATION TIME:
Less than 30 minutes
(plus baking time)

This is an attractive and filling casserole, and a meal in itself.

Preheat oven to 350 degrees. Sauté the onion, pepper, and garlic over low heat for about 15 minutes or until soft, then combine with remaining ingredients in a baking dish and bake 25 minutes.

Serves 4 to 6

170	Calories
4.9 g	Protein
29.7 g	Carbohydrates
3.6 g	Fat
19%	Calories from Fat
1.8 g	Fiber
90 mg	Sodium
8 mg	Cholesterol

Cooking with Herbs

Red Snapper with Salmoriglio

๛ ๛

1 tablespoon salt
2 tablespoons fresh lemon
    juice
1 teaspoon lemon zest
1 teaspoon fresh oregano,
    or ½ teaspoon dried
⅓ cup plus 2 tablespoons
    olive oil for rubbing
    on fish
¼ teaspoon pepper
2 cloves garlic, minced
2 pounds red snapper

PREPARATION TIME:
Less than 30 minutes

This is a Sicilian dish, although in Italy they use the sauce on a variety of fish. Try it with perch or other firm fish.

Dissolve salt in lemon juice, then add the zest and oregano and stir. Slowly add the ⅓ cup of olive oil, whisking it into the lemon juice so that it blends in as you go. Add the pepper. Combine the remaining oil with the garlic. Rub the fish with olive oil and garlic mix. Place in a nonstick baking pan and broil about 5 inches from heat until browned on both sides. Pour the sauce generously over the cooked fish.

Serves 4

441	Calories
45.3 g	Protein
1.3 g	Carbohydrates
27.7 g	Fat
56%	Calories from Fat
0.0 g	Fiber
1694 mg	Sodium
81 mg	Cholesterol

Onion Oregano Bread

2 tablespoons olive oil
½ cup chopped onion
1½ cups warm water
1 envelope dry yeast
½ teaspoon sugar
4½ cups flour
2 teaspoons salt
¼ cup fresh chopped
  oregano
1 egg, beaten with
  1 tablespoon water

PREPARATION TIME:
Over 1 hour

Here's a bread that is wonderful with soups, plus it smells so good as it bakes.

Heat the oil in a skillet and sauté the onion until soft, about 6 minutes. Remove from heat and cool. Pour the warm water into a small bowl, stir in yeast and sugar, and let stand until foamy, about 10 minutes.

Mix 4 cups of the flour with the salt. Stir in the cooked onion, then add the yeast mixture and fresh oregano. Mix well. Knead just until dough comes together, then turn out onto floured surface. Knead until smooth and elastic, adding flour as necessary to keep from sticking. This should take about 10 minutes.

Oil a bowl, then add the dough and turn to coat. Cover and let rise in a warm area for about 1 hour, until doubled in size. Punch down dough, then turn out onto a floured surface and knead briefly. Divide into two equal 6-inch round loaves. Place on an oiled baking sheet, cover with a towel again, and let rise until doubled, about 40 minutes.

Preheat oven to 450 degrees and brush each loaf with some of the beaten egg. Bake 10 minutes, reduce oven to 350 degrees, and bake about 35 minutes. Cool before serving.

Makes 2 loaves

152 Calories
4.2 g Protein
27.5 g Carbohydrates
2.4 g Fat
14% Calories from Fat
1.0 g Fiber
271 mg Sodium
13 mg Cholesterol

Nutritional analysis reflects the breakdown on 1 slice of bread.

Cooking with Herbs

PARSLEY

Romans wore parsley around their necks to ward off intoxication. (Since they also had numerous hangover remedies, it's safe to assume it was ineffective.) The Ancient Greeks believed parsley gave one stamina, and fed it to their horses.

Parsley is a native of the celery family. Both Greeks and Romans used it as a flavoring and garnish as early as the third century. Parsley provides plenty of vitamins A and C and is valued by herbalists to treat urinary infections and fluid retention. Parsley, a strong diuretic, has been shown to increase mother's milk and fight gout, although it is not recommended for medicinal use among pregnant women. Parsley has also been used as a breath freshener and to relieve allergies.

There really isn't any reason to use dried parsley when fresh is readily available and keeps quite a while in the refrigerator. Long used as simply a garnish in America, parsley has plenty of good uses in foods:

- Add to barbecue sauce, especially for poultry.
- Use in fish sauces and over fish.

- Add to dressings and vinaigrettes.
- Mix into butter and use parsley-butter on rice, potatoes, and vegetables.
- Stir into soups, especially minestrone.
- Sprinkle over vegetable sautés.
- Add to pasta dishes, especially cream sauces and lasagna.
- Mix into cheeses; stir into omelets.
- Combine with stuffings.
- Add to potato and other vegetable salads.

Cooking with Herbs

Corn Salad with Shrimp

Salad

3 cups cooked corn
½ sweet red pepper, diced
½ sweet green pepper, diced
1½ cups tiny cooked shrimp
½ cucumber, peeled, seeded, and diced

Dressing

2 tablespoons white wine vinegar
¼ cup chopped parsley
½ teaspoon minced thyme
Dash hot pepper sauce, or to taste
3½ tablespoons olive oil

PREPARATION TIME:
Less than 30 minutes

Vegetarians may omit the shrimp and still enjoy a delicious summer salad.

Combine the corn, peppers, shrimp, and cucumber in a bowl. Whisk the remaining ingredients together, then pour over the salad and toss.

Serves 4 to 6

175	Calories
9.3 g	Protein
18.1 g	Carbohydrates
8.6 g	Fat
44%	Calories from Fat
2.3 g	Fiber
78 mg	Sodium
63 mg	Cholesterol

Gruyère Rice Stuffed Peppers

❧ ❧

6 large sweet peppers, red or green, topped and seeded
¼ cup minced onion
2 tablespoons butter
4 cups cooked rice
½ cup chopped parsley
1 teaspoon fresh thyme, or ½ teaspoon dried
1 cup freshly grated Gruyère cheese
¼ cup chicken stock

PREPARATION TIME:
Less than 30 minutes
(plus baking time)

Trying to get my kids to enjoy vegetables is never especially easy. They do like cheese, however, and they always welcome these peppers.

Preheat oven to 325 degrees. Blanch the peppers in boiling water for 4 or 5 minutes. Remove and rinse. Heat butter and sauté onion over low heat until soft, about 10 minutes. Combine the onions with the rice, parsley, thyme, and cheese. Stir in the stock to mix. Place the peppers in an oiled baking dish, fill them with the rice mixture, pour ¼ cup water on the bottom of the dish, and bake 15 to 20 minutes.

Serves 6

316	Calories
10.4 g	Protein
44.1 g	Carbohydrates
10.7 g	Fat
30%	Calories from Fat
2.2 g	Fiber
115 mg	Sodium
32 mg	Cholesterol

Cooking with Herbs

Garlic and Hot Pepper Pasta

1 pound spaghetti or other
   pasta
¼ cup extra-virgin olive oil
3 cloves garlic, peeled
1 teaspoon seeded and
   minced serrano or
   jalapeño
⅓ cup chopped parsley
   Pepper
   Fresh grated cheese
   (optional)

PREPARATION TIME:
Less than 30 minutes

This quick pasta dish is spicy and good for you, with plenty of garlic and parsley. Serve with bread.

Cook pasta according to package directions. Place oil in a skillet, then add garlic and cook over medium-low heat until garlic is brown. Discard garlic; add the hot pepper and cook 2 minutes longer. Remove from heat; toss with pasta. Add parsley and toss again. Top with fresh pepper and cheese, if desired.

Serves 4 to 6

379	Calories
10.2 g	Protein
60.3 g	Carbohydrates
10.5 g	Fat
25%	Calories from Fat
3.5 g	Fiber
4 mg	Sodium
0 mg	Cholesterol

Minestrone with Parsley Pesto

❦ ❦

Soup

1 (16-ounce) can tomatoes
   with juice, or 2 fresh
   tomatoes
1 clove garlic, minced
2 tablespoons fresh
   shredded basil, or
   1 tablespoon dried
2 tablespoons olive oil
1 tablespoon butter, or
   another tablespoon of oil
2 onions, finely chopped
1 cup dried and cooked, or
   canned cannelli beans,
   drained
2 carrots, diced
1 zucchini, diced
2 potatoes, peeled and
   diced
1 cup shredded cabbage
1 cup green beans, trimmed
   and cut into pieces
2 teaspoons dried thyme
1 teaspoon dried oregano
¼ teaspoon pepper
⅛ teaspoon salt
1 cup orzo or other small
   pasta, cooked and
   drained
   Parmesan cheese
   (optional)

PREPARATION TIME:
Less than 1 hour
(plus simmer time)

Winter in Oregon can be dreary, calling for the invigorating taste of a hearty soup. This is a soup that will get you through the coldest day.

To make the soup, purée the tomatoes with garlic and basil and set aside. In a pot, heat oil and add onions. Cook until soft, about 6 minutes, then add beans, carrots, and zucchini and cook another 5 minutes. Add potatoes, cabbage, green beans, spices, tomato purée, and 4 quarts of water. Bring to a boil, cover, and simmer until beans are soft, about 90 minutes, stirring occasionally. Stir in the orzo, cover, and cook another 5 to 10 minutes, stirring frequently. Top each serving with parsley pesto, and grated Parmesan if desired.

To make the pesto, place all ingredients in a blender or processor and purée. Do not heat; simply stir in 1 to 2 tablespoons of the water from the pasta to warm.

Serves 6

Pesto

3 cups (packed) fresh
   chopped parsley
½ cup pine nuts
3 cloves garlic, minced
¼ teaspoon salt
⅓ cup olive oil

493	Calories
14.0 g	Protein
54.7 g	Carbohydrates
26.7 g	Fat
49%	Calories from Fat
6.8 g	Fiber
399 mg	Sodium
6 mg	Cholesterol

Cooking with Herbs

Summer Salad with Lemon Vinaigrette

❦ ❦

Salad

4 to 5 small zucchini, thinly sliced

1 small Vidalia or Walla Walla sweet onion, halved and thinly sliced

5 to 6 roma tomatoes, sliced

Vinaigrette

1/3 cup lemon juice

2 tablespoons lemon zest

2 tablespoons chopped parsley

2 teaspoons capers (optional)

1/2 teaspoon pepper, or to taste

1/4 teaspoon salt, or to taste

1/2 cup extra-virgin olive oil

PREPARATION TIME:
Less than 30 minutes

I came up with this fresh summer salad when the Walla Walla sweets were at their peak. I can never find too many uses for sweet onions.

Place the zucchini, onion, and tomatoes in a bowl. Whisk together the remaining ingredients, then add to vegetables and toss.

Serves 4

283	Calories
2.2 g	Protein
10.7 g	Carbohydrates
27.5 g	Fat
87%	Calories from Fat
2.6 g	Fiber
144 mg	Sodium
0 mg	Cholesterol

Lemon and Parsley Pasta Salad

½ pound orzo or other small pasta
2 tablespoons lemon juice
1 tablespoon lemon zest
¼ cup extra-virgin olive oil
¾ cup finely chopped parsley
½ cup Greek olives, pitted and halved

PREPARATION TIME:
Less than 30 minutes

An easy salad, one that I like chilled. Add a little feta cheese on top if you like.

Cook pasta according to package directions, drain, and allow to cool. Combine lemon juice, zest, oil, and parsley in a food processor or by hand until well mixed. Stir the dressing into the pasta and combine well. Top with olives and serve at room temperature or slightly chilled.

Serves 4

391	Calories
7.8 g	Protein
44.3 g	Carbohydrates
20.3 g	Fat
47%	Calories from Fat
2.0 g	Fiber
530 mg	Sodium
0 mg	Cholesterol

Cooking with Herbs

Carrots and Zucchini with Herb Sauce

1 pound carrots, sliced
2 zucchini, sliced
1 tablespoon Dijon mustard
1 teaspoon tarragon vinegar
3 tablespoons finely
    chopped parsley
1 teaspoon fresh tarragon,
    or ½ teaspoon dried
3 tablespoons extra-virgin
    olive oil
½ teaspoon lemon juice

PREPARATION TIME:
Less than 30 minutes

This is a simple vegetable mixture that goes especially well with roasts.

Combine the carrots and zucchini and steam until crisp-tender, about 8 minutes. Mix the mustard, vinegar, parsley, and tarragon in a bowl. Slowly add olive oil, whisking it in to mix. Add the lemon juice and whisk thoroughly. Toss with carrots and zucchini.

Serves 4 to 6

104	Calories
1.4 g	Protein
9.3 g	Carbohydrates
7.3 g	Fat
63%	Calories from Fat
1.6 g	Fiber
121 mg	Sodium
0 mg	Cholesterol

Tabbouleh

1 cup bulgur
1 onion, finely chopped
½ red bell pepper, seeded
and minced
3 green onions, finely
chopped
1 cup chopped parsley
½ cup chopped cilantro
⅓ cup fresh, finely chopped
mint
¼ cup extra-virgin olive oil
¼ cup lemon juice
1 teaspoon salt
1 teaspoon pepper
2 tomatoes, seeded and
chopped

PREPARATION TIME:
Less than 30 minutes
(plus sitting time
and chilling time)

*This Middle Eastern staple is very easy to make, but it does
need time to absorb the moisture and to chill. Serve alongside
or inside Pitas with Baba Ghanooj.*

Cover the bulgur with cold water and let stand until softened,
about 2½ hours. Line a strainer with a double layer of cheesecloth and pour in the bulgur. Twist the cloth and squeeze until all
moisture has been removed. Place the bulgur in a large bowl and
mix in the onion, bell peppers, and green onions. Stir in the parsley, cilantro, mint, oil, lemon juice, salt, and pepper. Add the
tomatoes. Cover and refrigerate 2 hours before serving.

Serves 4 to 6

190	Calories
4.1 g	Protein
24.5 g	Carbohydrates
9.7 g	Fat
46%	Calories from Fat
4.6 g	Fiber
374 mg	Sodium
0 mg	Cholesterol

Herbed Cream Cheese

১৯ ৫১

1 tablespoon wine or herb
   vinegar
1 clove garlic, minced
4 tablespoons chopped green
   onions
1 tablespoon chopped parsley
1 pound natural cream
   cheese

PREPARATION TIME:
Less than 30 minutes

Try adding a little of this to your scrambled eggs. If you are using commercial cream cheese, use a whipped style and add a little cream to make it smoother. This works well with goat cheese as well.

Combine the vinegar, garlic, green onions, and parsley well, using a food processor or by hand. Place cheese in a bowl and mix in the herb mixture well.

Makes about 1 1/2 cups

68	Calories
1.2 g	Protein
0.8 g	Carbohydrates
6.7 g	Fat
89%	Calories from Fat
0.0 g	Fiber
58 mg	Sodium
21 mg	Cholesterol

Four-Herb Tortellini

❧ ❧

¾ cup olive oil
⅓ cup chopped parsley
¼ cup finely chopped basil
2 tablespoons fresh, finely
  chopped dill, or
  1 teaspoon dried
2 tablespoons fresh, finely
  chopped marjoram, or
  1 teaspoon dried
3 cloves garlic, minced
½ teaspoon pepper
1 pound tortellini
2 green onions
  Parmesan cheese
  (optional)

PREPARATION TIME:
Less than 30 minutes
(plus marinating time)

These are the herbs I use when I make this dish. Substitute freely to please your palate.

Combine olive oil, parsley, basil, dill, marjoram, garlic, and pepper. Set aside to marinate 30 minutes. Cook tortellini according to package directions. Top with sauce and green onions, adding cheese if desired.

Serves 4 to 6

464	Calories
11.7 g	Protein
36.6 g	Carbohydrates
30.8 g	Fat
60%	Calories from Fat
2.6 g	Fiber
749 mg	Sodium
0 mg	Cholesterol

Green Onions and Tomatoes in Raspberry Vinaigrette

8 ripe tomatoes, sliced
3 green onions, thinly sliced
1/3 cup chopped parsley
3 tablespoons raspberry
　　vinegar

PREPARATION TIME:
Less than 30 minutes

I like this for picnics. The flavors here are as fresh as spring.

Toss the tomatoes, green onions, and parsley, then sprinkle with raspberry vinegar.

Serves 4

59	Calories
2.4 g	Protein
13.2 g	Carbohydrates
0.9 g	Fat
13%	Calories from Fat
3.6 g	Fiber
26 mg	Sodium
0 mg	Cholesterol

ROSEMARY

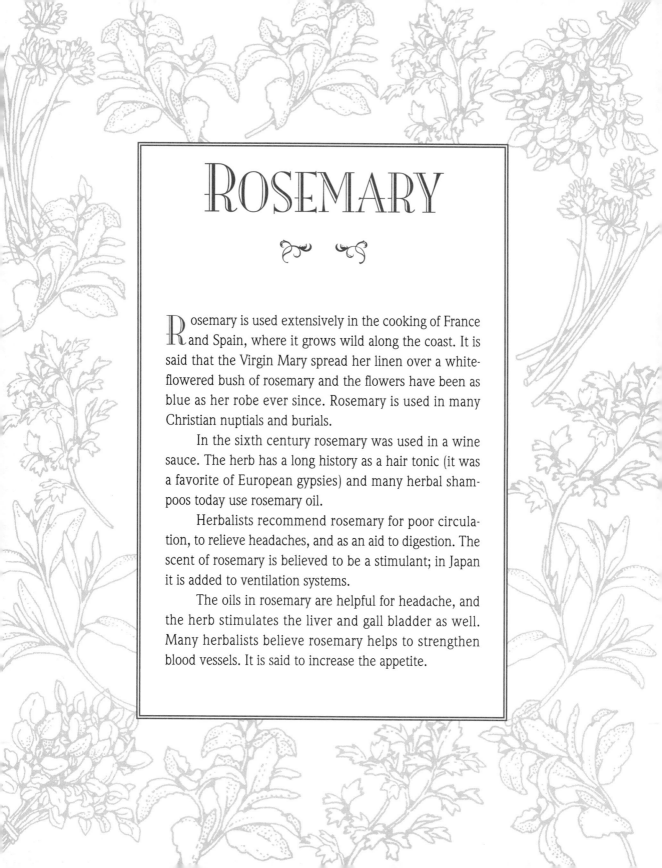

Rosemary is used extensively in the cooking of France and Spain, where it grows wild along the coast. It is said that the Virgin Mary spread her linen over a white-flowered bush of rosemary and the flowers have been as blue as her robe ever since. Rosemary is used in many Christian nuptials and burials.

In the sixth century rosemary was used in a wine sauce. The herb has a long history as a hair tonic (it was a favorite of European gypsies) and many herbal shampoos today use rosemary oil.

Herbalists recommend rosemary for poor circulation, to relieve headaches, and as an aid to digestion. The scent of rosemary is believed to be a stimulant; in Japan it is added to ventilation systems.

The oils in rosemary are helpful for headache, and the herb stimulates the liver and gall bladder as well. Many herbalists believe rosemary helps to strengthen blood vessels. It is said to increase the appetite.

Rosemary is culinary magic. I love the smell of it on my hands after using the fresh herb. Here are things I do with rosemary:

- Cook with soups, or add a little fresh rosemary sprinkled in late.
- Sprinkle over vegetables including peas, zucchini, beans, and especially potatoes.
- Cook with meats, especially pork and lamb.
- Add to stews, especially meat stews.
- Add to omelets and other egg dishes.
- Use with broiled fish, especially halibut and salmon.
- Rub on chicken before roasting.
- Add to breads and muffins.

Cooking with Herbs

Wild Rice Salad with Rosemary

½ cup toasted pine nuts
5 cups cooked white or
   brown rice
3 cups cooked wild rice
2 cups chopped chives or
   green onions
½ cup chopped parsley
¼ cup chopped mint
¼ cup fresh minced
   rosemary
¼ cup sun-dried tomatoes
¼ cup fresh lemon juice
¼ cup extra-virgin olive oil

PREPARATION TIME:
Less than 30 minutes
(plus time for cooking rice)

This salad goes well with fish dishes. Or serve with barbecue.

Combine all ingredients. Serve warm or chilled.

Serves 7 to 8

354	Calories
9.2 g	Protein
53.4 g	Carbohydrates
12.6 g	Fat
32%	Calories from Fat
2.4 g	Fiber
42 mg	Sodium
0 mg	Cholesterol

Penne in Rosemary Cream

12 ounces penne or other pasta
1 sprig fresh rosemary
8 tablespoons (1 stick) butter
3 tablespoons cream
1 tablespoon all-purpose flour
¼ cup Parmesan cheese

PREPARATION TIME:
Less than 30 minutes

This is definitely not lowfat, but it is one of my favorite splurge foods.

Cook pasta according to package directions. Melt butter over low heat in a skillet and add the rosemary sprig. Leave over very low heat for 20 minutes, stirring frequently to turn the butter into rosemary butter. Remove the rosemary sprig and any loose leaves and stir in the cream to mix. Add the flour, mix well, then stir in the cheese. Toss with the pasta.

Serves 4

559 Calories
12.9 g Protein
62.1 g Carbohydrates
28.7 g Fat
46% Calories from Fat
5.7 g Fiber
345 mg Sodium
74 mg Cholesterol

Cooking with Herbs

Lemon–Rosemary Chicken

꙳ ꙳

1 lemon
2 tablespoons olive oil
1 teaspoon minced plus
    1 sprig fresh rosemary
1 tablespoon fresh minced
    parsley
1 tablespoon fresh minced
    thyme
½ teaspoon fresh minced
    marjoram, or
    ¼ teaspoon dried
¼ teaspoon salt
½ teaspoon pepper
1 (3 to 3½ pound) fryer

PREPARATION TIME:
Less than 30 minutes
(plus roasting time)

Rosemary, so refreshing, smells wonderful as it cooks in this chicken.

Preheat oven to 450 degrees. Remove 2 teaspoons lemon zest from the lemon. Remove the peel from the lemon; cut into quarters. Place the lemon and the extra sprig of rosemary inside the chicken. Combine the lemon zest, minced rosemary, herbs, salt, and pepper and crush together into a paste, using a mortar and pestle or a small bowl and the back of a wooden spoon. Rub the mixture on the outside of the chicken. Tie drumsticks to tail and twist wings under back.

Place the chicken, breast side down, on a rack in a shallow roasting pan. Roast for 25 minutes, turn, and roast another 30 minutes until done. Remove rosemary and lemon from cavity.

Serves 4 to 6

291	Calories
28.6 g	Protein
0.3 g	Carbohydrates
18.7 g	Fat
58%	Calories from Fat
0.1 g	Fiber
175 mg	Sodium
92 mg	Cholesterol

Rosemary Focaccia

1 package (2½ teaspoons) dry active yeast

2 teaspoons sugar

1 cup warm water

2 tablespoons extra-virgin olive oil

1 teaspoon salt

3 cups all-purpose or bread flour

2 tablespoons fresh rosemary leaves, and/or other herbs

PREPARATION TIME: More than 1 hour

415 Calories
10.4 g Protein
74.5 g Carbohydrates
7.8 g Fat
17% Calories from Fat
2.5 g Fiber
537 mg Sodium
0 mg Cholesterol

I especially like my focaccia with rosemary leaves. You can also use this focaccia bread for pizza. Simply brush the top with your homemade tomato sauce, sprinkle with cheese and herbs, and toss on other toppings of your choice.

Place the yeast in a bowl. Stir in the sugar and water and set aside until bubbles appear, about 5 minutes. Stir in half the olive oil, the salt, and 1 cup of flour. Mix well, then stir in the remainder of the flour, ½ cup at a time. Turn the dough out onto a lightly floured surface and knead about 10 minutes, dusting whenever the dough gets too sticky. When it's smooth and elastic roll it into a ball.

Rub a clean bowl with 1 teaspoon of the remaining oil and roll the dough in the bowl until coated. Cover with a towel and set aside in a warm place to rise. It should double in size in about 90 minutes.

Preheat the oven to 475 degrees. Punch the dough down and divide it into four pieces. Shape each into a loaf about ½ inch thick. Place the loaves on a baking sheet, prick the surface with a fork, cover with a towel, and let rest 30 minutes. Brush loaves with the remaining olive oil and sprinkle with rosemary or other herbs. Bake about 15 minutes, until brown.

Makes 4 loaves

Nutritional analysis reflects breakdown of 1 loaf.

Cooking with Herbs

Rosemary Potatoes

2 pounds Russet potatoes
½ cup olive oil
1½ teaspoons salt
2 tablespoons fresh
    rosemary

PREPARATION TIME:
Less than 30 minutes
(plus baking time)

Rosemary goes well with potatoes. The vegetable takes on rosemary's oil and flavoring in this dish.

Preheat oven to 375 degrees. Scrub potatoes, then cut in half lengthwise. Cut into ¼-inch slices, taking care to make them the same thickness for even cooking. Coat potatoes with olive oil and salt. Place in a lightly oiled baking dish. Strew rosemary over potatoes. Cover; bake 30 minutes. Turn potatoes; bake 20 minutes longer.

Serves 4

440	Calories
4.3 g	Protein
46.6 g	Carbohydrates
27.3 g	Fat
56%	Calories from Fat
2.2 g	Fiber
813 mg	Sodium
0 mg	Cholesterol

Lemon–Garlic–Rosemary Chicken

2 boneless whole chicken breasts
4 large garlic cloves, chopped or minced
1 to 2 tablespoons finely chopped fresh rosemary
2 teaspoons lemon juice
2 tablespoons extra-virgin olive oil
Salt and pepper

PREPARATION TIME:
Less than 30 minutes

This is a summer favorite on the grill. I serve it with a spinach salad and corn on the cob.

Place chicken in a shallow glass dish. Toss with rosemary, garlic, lemon juice, olive oil, salt, and pepper. Let stand 15 to 30 minutes.

Grill about 3 to 4 minutes on each side.

Serves 4

207	Calories
26.9 g	Protein
1.3 g	Carbohydrates
9.9 g	Fat
43%	Calories from Fat
0.1 g	Fiber
64 mg	Sodium
73 mg	Cholesterol

Cooking with Herbs

SAGE

Sage has long been the symbol of wisdom and ancient herbalists believed it could strengthen memory. In the Middle Ages it was thought that sage could calm a fever, cure the common cold, and even fend off liver trouble.

There are more than 400 varieties of sage. The herb should always be stored in a cool place, since heat robs sage of flavor. Herbalists today use sage for sore throats, indigestion, and colds. Sage tea may help mouth ulcers to heal. Use sage tea combined with a little vinegar as a gargle for sore throats. Sage is believed to help the nervous system and is used by herbalists to treat the hot flashes of menopause. The herb also has a reputation for tempering sexual desire, and according to the Chinese, it stimulates mental alertness. To make sage tea, steep 2 teaspoons of fresh, chopped leaves in boiling water for 10 minutes. Remove leaves before serving. The Germans use this tea as a gargle for sore throats.

Sage has many culinary uses:

- Add to cream soups and chowders.
- Make sage butter to serve with broiled fish, poultry, or pork.
- Rub sage on meat before roasting, add to sausage, mix into meat gravies.
- Add to dumplings and stuffings.
- Use with lima beans, eggplant, tomatoes.
- Use a leaf in stews to give a hint of sage flavor.

Sage Applesauce

❦ ❧

4 pounds Cortland or other
    cooking apples
1/2 cup water
1/4 cup sage leaves

PREPARATION TIME:
Less than 30 minutes

It's easy to make your own applesauce. Make this with fresh sage only—dried sage won't work.

Peel, core, and quarter the apples, then place in a saucepan with the water and sage leaves. Cover and cook over medium-high heat for 15 minutes, until apples are soft. (Keep the heat down to make sure the apples do not stick to the pan.) Remove apples and let cool for 10 minutes or so. Discard sage. Place apples in a food processor and purée.

Makes about 3 quarts (1 cup per serving)

71	Calories
0.2 g	Protein
18.6 g	Carbohydrates
0.4 g	Fat
5%	Calories from Fat
2.4 g	Fiber
0 mg	Sodium
0 mg	Cholesterol

Sage and Fontina Chicken

2 teaspoons butter
2 teaspoons olive oil
2 whole boneless, skinless
   chicken breasts, halved
2 tablespoons fresh sage, or
   1 tablespoon dried
   (not ground)
½ teaspoon pepper
4 thin slices fontina cheese

PREPARATION TIME:
Less than 30 minutes

Sage tastes so good with poultry, not to mention butter and cheese. Here is a dish that marries all three.

Preheat the broiler. Melt the butter with the oil in a skillet. Add chicken breasts and cook over medium heat for 4 minutes. Turn, sprinkle with sage and pepper, and cook another 3 minutes. Do not overcook. Remove to a serving plate and place one slice of cheese on each piece of chicken. Place under the broiler just long enough to melt the cheese. Serve at once.

Serves 4

237	Calories
30.4 g	Protein
0.5 g	Carbohydrates
11.9 g	Fat
45%	Calories from Fat
0.0 g	Fiber
208 mg	Sodium
95 mg	Cholesterol

Asparagus Soup with Sage Pesto

1 tablespoon pine nuts
1 clove garlic, peeled
2 cups parsley
1/3 cup fresh sage leaves
2 tablespoons grated
    Parmesan
1 teaspoon white wine
    vinegar
4 tablespoons extra-virgin
    olive oil
2 tablespoons flour
5 cups vegetable or
    chicken stock
2 1/2 pounds asparagus, cut
    into pieces
1 teaspoon salt

PREPARATION TIME:
Less than 1 hour

I came upon this combination more by accident—having the pesto on hand when making the soup. It is a rich, delicious blend of vegetables and herbs.

In a food processor or blender, combine the pine nuts, garlic, parsley, sage, Parmesan, and vinegar and slowly add half the oil to form a purée. Heat the remaining oil in a pot and whisk in the flour, mixing until smooth. Whisk in the stock, bring to a boil, and add the asparagus and salt. Reduce heat and simmer, covered, for about 30 minutes. Remove to a food processor and purée. Reheat, then ladle into bowls and add a dollop of pesto on top.

Serves 4 to 6

287 Calories
8.8 g Protein
38.8 g Carbohydrates
11.4 g Fat
36% Calories from Fat
3.1 g Fiber
411 mg Sodium
1 mg Cholesterol

Lemon and Sage Rice

❧ ☙

1 cup basmati rice
1 tablespoon oil or butter
¼ cup minced onion
¼ cup chicken or vegetable
    stock
1 teaspoon fresh minced
    sage, or ½ teaspoon
    dried
   Juice and zest of 1 lemon
2 tablespoons chopped
    parsley

PREPARATION TIME:
Less than 30 minutes

Serve this alongside meats or fish dishes.

Heat a pot of water to boiling and add the rice, stirring to keep from sticking. Boil, uncovered, for 5 minutes. Meanwhile, melt the butter and sauté onion in oil or butter until soft, 3 to 4 minutes. Drain the rice and mix with the onion. Add the stock, sage, zest, and lemon juice and cook, stirring constantly, over medium-low heat until liquid has evaporated, 4 to 5 minutes. Stir in the parsley and serve.

Serves 4

210	Calories
3.7 g	Protein
39.7 g	Carbohydrates
3.9 g	Fat
17%	Calories from Fat
0.7 g	Fiber
9 mg	Sodium
0 mg	Cholesterol

Sage and Garlic Potatoes

୨୦ ୧ଓ

2 to 2½ pounds potatoes, peeled and halved

4 tablespoons olive oil

2 cloves garlic, peeled and thinly sliced

1½ tablespoons fresh minced sage, or 2 teaspoons dried

1 cup sour cream or yogurt

½ cup milk

PREPARATION TIME:
Less than 30 minutes

Potatoes have always been one of my comfort foods. Here is a new twist I created for my mashed potatoes. Make potato pancakes with the leftovers.

Boil the potatoes until cooked through, about 30 minutes. Meanwhile, in a saucepan, heat the oil and add the garlic. Cook over medium-low heat until golden, about 20 minutes. Add sage and remove from heat. Let stand 10 minutes, then strain the oil, discarding the garlic and sage leaves. Drain potatoes and mash. Stir the sage-garlic oil into the potatoes, then mix in remaining ingredients, adding more or less milk to achieve desired consistency.

Serves 4 to 6

288	Calories
4.3 g	Protein
32.4 g	Carbohydrates
16.3 g	Fat
51%	Calories from Fat
2.2 g	Fiber
34 mg	Sodium
15 mg	Cholesterol

Cooking with Herbs

SAVORY

❧   ❧

S avory, both the delicate tasting summer and the sharper winter variety, helps to bring out the natural flavors in foods. The Egyptians thought this southern Europe native to be an aphrodisiac.

Their names have no relation to what time of year they are produced; summer savory is used more frequently.

Savory helps to stimulate the appetite. If you are using winter savory, use a little less than what the recipe calls for.

You can add savory to many things:

- Try it in an omelet or other egg dish.
- Use it in place of parsley in a dish, using slightly less.
- Add just a little to salads and dressings, and especially to bean salads.
- Mix into soups, especially potato.
- Add to fish and fish sauces.
- Combine with your favorite stuffing recipes.
- Sprinkle over vegetables including green beans, peas, and zucchini.
- Stir into rice before serving.
- Good with poultry, and roasts.
- Make a savory tea by steeping 2 teaspoons in boiling water.

Orzo with Fresh Herbs and Vegetables

8 ounces orzo
1 tablespoon olive oil
1 cup diced zucchini
1 cup diced bell pepper
½ cup diced onion
1 small clove garlic, minced
1 teaspoon fresh chopped
   savory
2 teaspoons fresh herbs
   (basil, sorrel, thyme,
   parsley)
   Parmesan cheese
   (optional)

PREPARATION TIME:
Less than 30 minutes

This recipe is best with summer savory. Substitute basil or parsley when savory isn't available.

Cook pasta according to package directions. In a skillet, heat oil and sauté the zucchini, bell pepper, and onion until softened, about 7 minutes. Add garlic, cook 3 more minutes, and remove from heat. Combine the orzo, vegetables, and herbs in a bowl. Stir in Parmesan cheese, if desired.

Serves 4

263	Calories
8.0 g	Protein
46.2 g	Carbohydrates
4.5 g	Fat
16%	Calories from Fat
2.8 g	Fiber
2 mg	Sodium
0 mg	Cholesterol

Green Beans Provençal

1 pound green beans
1 tablespoon olive oil
1 onion, sliced
4 tomatoes, peeled and
    chopped
2 cloves garlic, minced
1 teaspoon minced savory
1 tablespoon minced parsley

PREPARATION TIME:
Less than 1 hour

Simple, straightforward vegetables prepared in the style of southern France.

Blanch the green beans in boiling water 4 to 5 minutes, then rinse in cold water to stop cooking. Heat oil and sauté onion for 3 minutes. Add the tomatoes for a minute more, then add the garlic and savory. Reduce to low, cover, and cook for 15 minutes. Add the green beans and cook another 15 minutes. Stir in the parsley and serve.

Serves 4 to 6

73	Calories
2.4 g	Protein
11.6 g	Carbohydrates
2.8 g	Fat
35%	Calories from Fat
2.7 g	Fiber
10 mg	Sodium
0 mg	Cholesterol

Chicken with Savory in Tomato Sauce

꿍 꿎

5 tablespoons olive oil
1 (2½-pound) chicken, cut
    into parts
2 onions, sliced
2 cloves garlic, minced
½ cup dry white wine
2 cups tomato sauce (home-
    made recommended)
3 sprigs savory

PREPARATION TIME:
Less than 1 hour
(plus baking time)

Here is a delicious entrée, filling and healthful. A great Sunday dinner.

In a skillet, heat 2 tablespoons of oil and brown half the chicken on both sides for about 10 minutes. Add 2 tablespoons oil and brown remaining chicken. Reduce heat and sauté onions and garlic until soft in remaining oil, about 5 minutes. Transfer the chicken, onions, and garlic to a Dutch oven. Preheat oven to 325 degrees. Pour the wine into the skillet and bring to a boil, scraping the bottom of the pan. Add the tomato sauce and cook another minute or two. Pour mixture over the chicken and add savory alongside the chicken. Cover and cook 90 minutes, turning once during the cooking process.

Serves 4 to 6

373	Calories
27.8 g	Protein
9.7 g	Carbohydrates
24.4 g	Fat
59%	Calories from Fat
1.9 g	Fiber
573 mg	Sodium
84 mg	Cholesterol

Cooking with Herbs

Green Bean Salad with Savory

୧୬ ୬୧

1 pound green beans, cut into pieces

1/3 sweet onion, thinly sliced and halved

1/3 cup extra-virgin olive oil

1 1/2 tablespoons red wine vinegar

1 teaspoon minced fresh oregano

1 tablespoon minced fresh savory

1/2 teaspoon pepper

PREPARATION TIME:
Less than 30 minutes (plus standing time)

This is an easy and different side dish, or good as part of a salad plate. I also have it on my list for picnics.

Steam the beans until crisp-tender, about 4 minutes. Rinse under cold water to stop cooking. Place in a medium bowl and cool for 10 minutes. Add remaining ingredients and mix well. Let stand 20 minutes. Serve at room temperature.

Serves 4 to 6

134	Calories
1.5 g	Protein
6.7 g	Carbohydrates
12.1 g	Fat
81%	Calories from Fat
1.4 g	Fiber
2 mg	Sodium
0 mg	Cholesterol

Savory Corn Relish

⤳ ⤶

1 cup fresh or frozen corn,
  cooked
2 roasted red peppers,
  thinly sliced
¼ cup fresh summer savory
1 clove garlic, minced
¼ cup extra-virgin olive oil
  Juice from 1 lemon

PREPARATION TIME:
Less than 30 minutes

Try this quick relish with fish, in tortillas, or with Mexican foods.

Toss all ingredients together; cool.

Makes about 2$^1/_2$ cups (1 tablespoon per serving)

17	Calories
0.2 g	Protein
1.3 g	Carbohydrates
1.4 g	Fat
72%	Calories from Fat
0.1 g	Fiber
14 mg	Sodium
0 mg	Cholesterol

SORREL

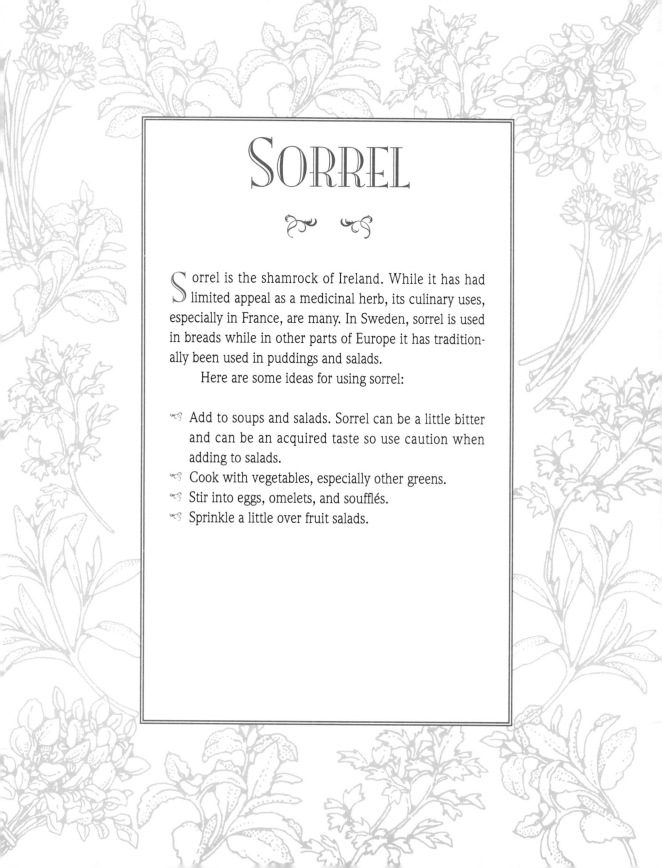

S orrel is the shamrock of Ireland. While it has had limited appeal as a medicinal herb, its culinary uses, especially in France, are many. In Sweden, sorrel is used in breads while in other parts of Europe it has traditionally been used in puddings and salads.

Here are some ideas for using sorrel:

- Add to soups and salads. Sorrel can be a little bitter and can be an acquired taste so use caution when adding to salads.
- Cook with vegetables, especially other greens.
- Stir into eggs, omelets, and soufflés.
- Sprinkle a little over fruit salads.

Sorrel Cream Sauce

❦ ❦

1 tablespoon butter
2 shallots, chopped
1½ cups dry white wine
1 cup cream
10 ounces sorrel (about 50 leaves)
10 ounces fresh spinach
1 teaspoon lemon juice
½ teaspoon lemon zest
¼ teaspoon salt
½ teaspoon pepper

PREPARATION TIME:
Less than 1 hour

This sauce is great with salmon, or try it with other fish or vegetables.

Sauté the shallots in the butter for 2 minutes. Add wine and cook down by half. Stir in cream, sorrel, and spinach and cook 5 minutes more. Add remaining ingredients, remove from heat, and allow to cool. Place the mixture in a blender or food processor until it becomes sauce-like, but not completely puréed. Serve warm or cold.

Makes about 2 cups (¼ cup per serving)

85	Calories
2.8 g	Protein
4.8 g	Carbohydrates
5.6 g	Fat
59%	Calories from Fat
1.2 g	Fiber
126 mg	Sodium
16 mg	Cholesterol

Cream of Sorrel Soup

2 tablespoons butter
1 cup chopped sweet onion
1 potato, peeled and diced
4 cups fresh chopped sorrel
4 cups chicken stock
1 egg yolk, beaten
½ teaspoon pepper sauce
¾ cup milk, half-and-half,
   or cream

PREPARATION TIME:
Less than 1 hour

A creamy soup, good with a green salad and bread. Sprinkle a touch of paprika on top for color.

Melt butter in a saucepan, add onion and potato, and cook over medium-low heat for 3 minutes. Add sorrel and stir until wilted. Add the stock and bring to a boil. Reduce heat and simmer 20 minutes. Remove from heat.

Purée the mixture in a food processor or blender, return to the pot, and add the egg yolk and pepper sauce. Turn heat to low and stir in the milk or cream. Serve warm, but do not boil.

Serves 4 to 6

120 Calories
5.5 g Protein
12.2 g Carbohydrates
6.2 g Fat
46% Calories from Fat
1.4 g Fiber
124 mg Sodium
49 mg Cholesterol

Tarragon

Tarragon is a native of Russia. In the Middle Ages tarragon was used as a treatment for toothache. It has essential oil and may help to stimulate the appetite, but few herbalists use tarragon now for medicinal purposes.

Tarragon's position as a culinary herb is assured, especially in French cuisine, where its slightly licorice flavor is used in many dishes. When growing tarragon be sure to use French tarragon for the best flavor.

Here are ways I use tarragon:

- Add to vinaigrettes and especially to mustard dressings. Mustard and tarragon are a natural marriage.
- Sprinkle into or cook with soups, especially chowders, chicken, tomato.
- Add to vegetable salads.
- Use with roasted poultry.
- Use in marinades for fish.
- Add to eggs and omelets.
- Add to cream sauces and tartar sauce.

Salmon with Walnut, Dill, and Tarragon

≈

¾ cup plain yogurt
¼ teaspoon salt
2 teaspoons fresh chopped
    dill
¼ teaspoon tarragon
½ teaspoon vinegar
1 teaspoon lemon juice
2 teaspoons walnut oil
1 teaspoon plus
    1 tablespoon chopped
    toasted walnuts
2 pounds salmon fillets,
    grilled or pan-fried

PREPARATION TIME:
Less than 30 minutes

Fresh tarragon and dill go well with fish. Use fresh herbs in this dish, not dried.

Combine all except the chopped walnuts and salmon in a blender and blend until smooth. Stir in chopped walnuts, then pour over fish.

Serves 4

422	Calories
51.2 g	Protein
4.4 g	Carbohydrates
20.9 g	Fat
45%	Calories from Fat
0.2 g	Fiber
273 mg	Sodium
134 mg	Cholesterol

Cooking with Herbs

Daikon and Red Pepper Salad
with Tarragon Vinaigrette

❧ ☙

Salad
½ to ¾ head leaf lettuce
1 small zucchini, thinly sliced
1 small red pepper, cut into matchsticks
½ sweet onion, thinly sliced
¾ cup thinly sliced daikon

Vinaigrette
3 tablespoons tarragon or red wine vinegar
1 teaspoon Dijon mustard
1½ teaspoons fresh minced tarragon, or
½ teaspoon dried
¼ teaspoon salt
¼ teaspoon pepper
7 tablespoons extra-virgin olive oil

PREPARATION TIME:
Less than 30 minutes

This colorful salad goes well with pasta dishes.

Tear the washed and dried lettuce and place in a salad bowl. Place the zucchini, red pepper, sweet onion, and daikon on top and toss. Combine the remaining ingredients, whisking in the olive oil a tablespoon at a time. Toss dressing with salad.

Serves 4 to 6

159	Calories
1.0 g	Protein
4.3 g	Carbohydrates
16.1 g	Fat
91%	Calories from Fat
0.9 g	Fiber
116 mg	Sodium
0 mg	Cholesterol

Lemon Linguine with Tarragon

½ pound linguine
1 small zucchini, sliced
½ cup extra-virgin olive oil
    Juice of ½ lemon
2 tablespoons lemon zest
2 tablespoons fresh
    chopped chives or
    green onions
3 tablespoons fresh, finely
    chopped tarragon
2 tablespoons fresh herbs
    (basil, marjoram, or
    parsley)

PREPARATION TIME:
Less than 30 minutes

I like the fresh taste of herbs and lemon with pasta. I generally serve this as a side dish or a lunch entrée.

Cook pasta according to package instructions, drain, and rinse. Steam sliced zucchini until crisp-tender, about 8 minutes. Toss with the pasta. Combine the oil, lemon juice, and lemon zest and pour over the pasta; add fresh herbs, and toss well. Add additional lemon juice if desired.

Serves 4

468 Calories
8.1 g Protein
47.0 g Carbohydrates
28.1 g Fat
54% Calories from Fat
3.0 g Fiber
2 mg Sodium
0 mg Cholesterol

Cooking with Herbs

Braised Carrots with Tarragon and Parsley

☙ ❧

1 pound carrots, peeled and
  cut into sticks
3 tablespoons olive oil
1 teaspoon salt
1 clove garlic, minced
1 tablespoon fresh minced
  tarragon
¼ cup minced parsley

PREPARATION TIME:
Less than 30 minutes

Here's a simple way to enjoy carrots with a dressing of fresh herbs and olive oil. I like this with poultry.

Heat the carrots, oil, and salt in a pan. Cover and simmer 15 minutes. Toss with garlic, tarragon, and parsley, cover, and braise 3 to 4 minutes. Remove to a bowl, boil down remaining juices, and pour over carrots.

Serves 4 to 6

89	Calories
0.8 g	Protein
6.9 g	Carbohydrates
6.9 g	Fat
69%	Calories from Fat
1.0 g	Fiber
398 mg	Sodium
0 mg	Cholesterol

Fresh Trout in Tarragon

❦

2 cloves garlic, minced
¼ teaspoon salt
¼ teaspoon pepper
½ cup extra-virgin olive oil
¼ cup lime juice
3 tablespoons fresh
   chopped tarragon
4 trout, cleaned

PREPARATION TIME:
Less than 30 minutes
(plus marinating time)

Tarragon complements the flavor of the fish. I like this with many rice dishes.

Whisk together marinade ingredients and pour over fish. Cover and refrigerate for 30 minutes or longer. Remove fish, reserving liquid. Grill 3 inches from heat, basting with marinade, 5 to 6 minutes per side.

Serves 4

385	Calories
40.2 g	Protein
1.8 g	Carbohydrates
23.7 g	Fat
55%	Calories from Fat
0.0 g	Fiber
165 mg	Sodium
121 mg	Cholesterol

Cooking with Herbs

Grilled Halibut in
Lemon–Mustard–Tarragon Marinade

½ cup fresh lemon juice

1 tablespoon minced lemon zest

¼ cup Dijon mustard (or half dill mustard and Dijon mustard)

3 tablespoons chopped tarragon

2 tablespoons chopped chives or green onions

¼ cup extra-virgin olive oil

¼ teaspoon freshly ground black pepper

6 (½-pound pieces) halibut steaks or fillets

PREPARATION TIME:
Less than 30 minutes (plus marinating time)

This is an absolute favorite during summer and has never failed to bring anything less than great reviews. Be careful not to over-cook the fish.

Combine lemon juice, zest, mustard, tarragon, and chives. Slowly whisk in olive oil. Add pepper. Place the fish in a shallow glass dish, add marinade to coat, and refrigerate for 1 hour. Barbecue over medium heat, about 3 inches from the flame, 5 minutes per side.

Serves 6

258	Calories
44.3 g	Protein
0.7 g	Carbohydrates
7.5 g	Fat
26%	Calories from Fat
0.0 g	Fiber
182 mg	Sodium
68 mg	Cholesterol

THYME

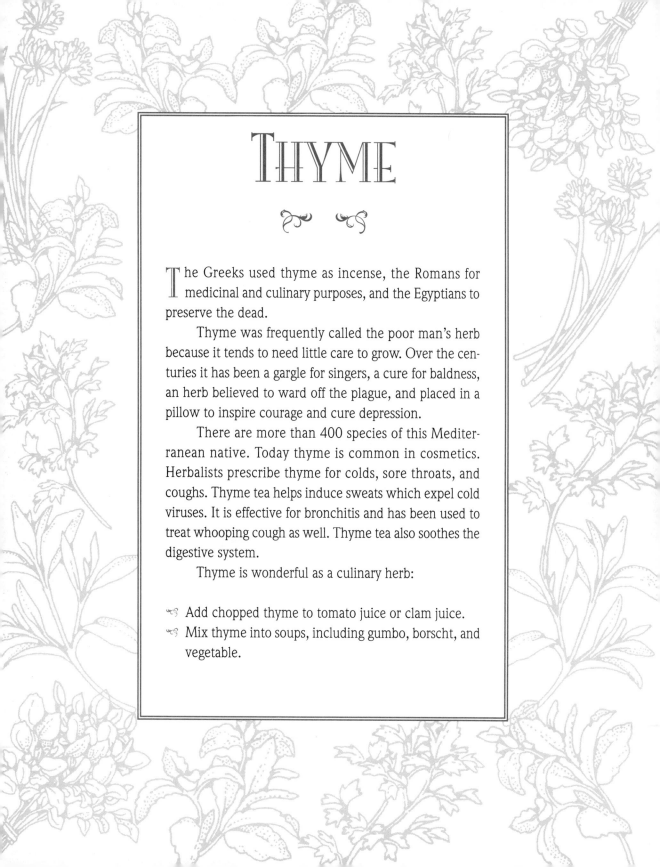

T he Greeks used thyme as incense, the Romans for medicinal and culinary purposes, and the Egyptians to preserve the dead.

Thyme was frequently called the poor man's herb because it tends to need little care to grow. Over the centuries it has been a gargle for singers, a cure for baldness, an herb believed to ward off the plague, and placed in a pillow to inspire courage and cure depression.

There are more than 400 species of this Mediterranean native. Today thyme is common in cosmetics. Herbalists prescribe thyme for colds, sore throats, and coughs. Thyme tea helps induce sweats which expel cold viruses. It is effective for bronchitis and has been used to treat whooping cough as well. Thyme tea also soothes the digestive system.

Thyme is wonderful as a culinary herb:

- Add chopped thyme to tomato juice or clam juice.
- Mix thyme into soups, including gumbo, borscht, and vegetable.

- Mix into dressings and salads.
- Thyme goes well with most fish and many fish marinades and sauces, or make a thyme butter.
- Use with vegetables, including carrots and beets, and sprinkle over vegetable sautés.
- Add to stuffings.
- Use with poultry, especially roast chicken.
- Add to stews, especially lamb.

Herbed Asparagus

1 pound asparagus
3 tablespoons butter or
   extra-virgin olive oil
3 tablespoons fresh minced
   chives or scallions
¼ teaspoon fresh minced
   thyme
1 teaspoon fresh minced
   parsley

PREPARATION TIME:
Less than 30 minutes

For me, the harbinger of spring is asparagus. I am a big fan of this vegetable, and this creation is a springtime treat.

Steam asparagus until done, 7 to 10 minutes. Melt butter and combine with the herbs, or mix the oil with the herbs, and pour over the asparagus.

Serves 4 to 6

73	Calories
2.0 g	Protein
3.2 g	Carbohydrates
6.4 g	Fat
78%	Calories from Fat
1.0 g	Fiber
70 mg	Sodium
17 mg	Cholesterol

Lemon–Thyme Fettuccine

1 pound fettuccine or other pasta
2 tablespoons olive oil
4 zucchini, sliced
2 tablespoons fresh chopped lemon thyme or thyme
3 to 4 cloves garlic, minced
Juice of 1½ lemons
1 cup fresh grated Parmesan or pecorino cheese

PREPARATION TIME:
Less than 30 minutes

Lemon and pasta are an unusual combination, but they go well in this mix.

Cook pasta according to package directions. Heat olive oil in a skillet and add zucchini. Cook over medium heat about 7 minutes; add thyme and cook another 3 minutes. Add garlic, stir and cook 2 minutes, then pour in the lemon juice and remove from heat. Toss with cooked and drained pasta; top with cheese.

Serves 4

619	Calories
24.7 g	Protein
95.9 g	Carbohydrates
15.0 g	Fat
22%	Calories from Fat
6.3 g	Fiber
378 mg	Sodium
16 mg	Cholesterol

Cooking with Herbs

Parmesan Chicken with Thyme

½ cup flour
½ teaspoon salt, or to taste
¼ teaspoon pepper, or to taste
½ teaspoon fresh minced thyme, or ¼ teaspoon dried
½ cup fine bread crumbs
½ cup fresh grated Parmesan
1 tablespoon olive oil
2 whole skinless, boneless chicken breasts, halved
2 eggs, beaten

PREPARATION TIME:
Less than 30 minutes

A simple chicken dish, with thyme providing much of the flavor. Thyme is always good with chicken.

Combine the flour, salt, pepper, and thyme in a bowl. Combine the bread crumbs and Parmesan (this may be done in a food processor) in a separate bowl. Heat oil in a skillet over medium-low heat. Dip the chicken into the flour and spice mixture to coat, dip into the beaten eggs, then into the Parmesan and bread crumbs bowl. Cook 5 minutes on one side and 2 to 3 on the other, until just cooked through.

Serves 4

357	Calories
36.5 g	Protein
22.6 g	Carbohydrates
12.1 g	Fat
31%	Calories from Fat
0.7 g	Fiber
635 mg	Sodium
163 mg	Cholesterol

Asparagus and Red Pepper Penne

❧ ❧

¾ pound penne
1 tablespoon butter
1 tablespoon olive oil
¾ pound asparagus, cut into
    pieces, steamed
    crisp-tender
3 red peppers, roasted and
    diced
1 clove garlic, minced
1 tablespoon fresh minced
    thyme, or 1 teaspoon
    dried
  Parmesan cheese
  (optional)

PREPARATION TIME:
Less than 30 minutes

This colorful dish is a meal by itself. Use a good-quality cheese for terrific results.

Cook the pasta according to package instructions, then drain and rinse. Heat butter and olive oil over medium-high heat and add asparagus. Stir until browned or blackened, about 7 minutes. Remove from heat, stir in the red peppers and garlic, and allow the heat from the pan to cook the peppers and garlic. Return to low heat for a minute or two (if needed to cook the pepper), stirring to prevent the garlic from burning. Combine the pasta with the pepper mixture, and sprinkle on thyme. Toss to mix well and serve with Parmesan, if desired.

Serves 4 to 6

256	Calories
8.4 g	Protein
43.5 g	Carbohydrates
5.6 g	Fat
20%	Calories from Fat
4.8 g	Fiber
168 mg	Sodium
6 mg	Cholesterol

Cooking with Herbs

Corn and Potato Soup with Thyme

❧ ❧

1 tablespoon olive oil
1 onion, chopped
1 (15-ounce) can vegetable
    or chicken broth
1 potato, peeled and diced
2 cups corn, fresh or frozen
2 tablespoons fresh chopped
    thyme, or 2 teaspoons
    dried
½ teaspoon salt
½ teaspoon pepper
1 cup milk

PREPARATION TIME:
Less than 30 minutes

A quick chowder that is good at lunch, for a barbecue, or in a cup on the side. Use fresh corn for best results.

Heat oil and sauté onion until soft, about 5 minutes. Add broth and potato, cover, and simmer 5 minutes more. Add corn, thyme, salt, and pepper and bring to a boil; reduce heat, partially cover pan, and simmer until vegetables are tender, about 10 minutes. Add milk and warm 4 or 5 minutes more.

Serves 4 to 6

119	Calories
4.2 g	Protein
19.8 g	Carbohydrates
3.4 g	Fat
26%	Calories from Fat
1.9 g	Fiber
229 mg	Sodium
3 mg	Cholesterol

Lemon–Thyme Chicken and Orzo Soup

୧ ୧

1 teaspoon olive oil
2 carrots, thinly sliced
½ onion, chopped
2 stalks celery, sliced
8 cups chicken stock
  Zest of ½ lemon
2 teaspoons fresh thyme, or
  1 teaspoon dried
1 cup cooked orzo or other
  small pasta, or cooked
  rice
2 cups cooked chicken,
  shredded

PREPARATION TIME:
Less than 30 minutes
(plus cooking time)

This is another comforting soup, one that you'll wish your mother had made for you. Poach the chicken or use leftovers.

Heat the oil and sauté the carrots, onion, and celery until soft, about 8 minutes. Add stock, zest, and thyme and cook over low heat for about 1 hour. Add the orzo and chicken and cook another few minutes, until heated through.

Serves 4 to 6

240	Calories
20.8 g	Protein
30.3 g	Carbohydrates
3.2 g	Fat
12%	Calories from Fat
1.6 g	Fiber
177 mg	Sodium
35 mg	Cholesterol

Honey-Thyme Acorn Squash

৵৵ ৵৵

1 acorn squash, seeded and
    cut into pieces
1 cup water
2 tablespoons butter, melted
2 tablespoons lemon juice
1 teaspoon fresh chopped
    thyme, or ½ teaspoon
    dried
2 teaspoons honey

PREPARATION TIME:
Less than 1 hour

Make sure the squash is nice and tender for all of its sweetness to come out. A great fall soup.

Place the squash in a pot with the water and bring to a boil. Reduce heat to low, cover, and simmer until tender, about 25 minutes. Add the remaining ingredients and cook, mixing well, for about 5 minutes to blend flavors.

Serves 4 to 6

71	Calories
1.1 g	Protein
8.7 g	Carbohydrates
4.2 g	Fat
53%	Calories from Fat
1.3 g	Fiber
44 mg	Sodium
11 mg	Cholesterol

Zucchini with Herbs and Sour Cream

2   tablespoons butter
5   small zucchini, trimmed
    and thinly sliced
½   teaspoon salt
⅛   cup lemon juice
1   tablespoon fresh, finely
    minced thyme, or
    1 teaspoon dried
1   tablespoon fresh, finely
    minced dill, or
    1 teaspoon dried
¾   cup sour cream

PREPARATION TIME:
Less than 30 minutes

You can use other vegetables with this, but I think zucchini is best. An easy side dish to simple meat entrées, or as part of a vegetable plate.

In a skillet, melt the butter and add the zucchini. Sprinkle with salt, lemon juice, and herbs and sauté over low heat for 6 minutes, until just crisp-tender. Fold the sour cream into the mixture and warm but do not cook.

Serves 4

152	Calories
2.7 g	Protein
5.9 g	Carbohydrates
13.8 g	Fat
82%	Calories from Fat
1.5 g	Fiber
349 mg	Sodium
32 mg	Cholesterol

Linguine with Tapenade

❧ ❧

1 cup pitted Niçoise olives
1 pound linguine or other pasta
3 tablespoons capers
10 to 12 leaves fresh basil
2 cloves garlic, minced
¾ teaspoon fresh thyme, or ¼ teaspoon dried
2 tablespoons lemon juice
½ teaspoon freshly ground pepper
6 tablespoons olive oil

PREPARATION TIME:
Less than 30 minutes

It is unusual to toss a tapenade with pasta, since this Provençal staple is generally used with meats and on bread. It is a dish not for the faint of heart, and one I generally serve as a side dish, not an entrée.

Cook pasta according to package directions. Put remaining ingredients in food processor and chop to mix well but do not purée. Toss with pasta.

Serves 4 to 6

458	Calories
10.6 g	Protein
64.0 g	Carbohydrates
18.3 g	Fat
36%	Calories from Fat
4.5 g	Fiber
327 mg	Sodium
0 mg	Cholesterol

Herbed Chickpea Salad

❦ ❧

2 tablespoons red wine vinegar

2 tablespoons fresh lemon juice

3 cloves garlic, minced

6 tablespoons extra-virgin olive oil

½ teaspoon pepper

¼ teaspoon salt

2 cups cooked or canned chickpeas, rinsed and drained

¼ cup pitted black olives

½ sweet onion, diced

1 tablespoon fresh thyme, or 1 teaspoon dried

2 teaspoons fresh rosemary, or 1 teaspoon dried

1 teaspoon fresh tarragon, or ½ teaspoon dried

1 teaspoon fresh oregano, or ½ teaspoon dried

PREPARATION TIME:
Less than 30 minutes

Chickpeas are almost always associated with Middle Eastern foods, and this goes well with those. But I like to serve it with barbecue and meat dishes as well.

Combine the vinegar, lemon juice, garlic, olive oil, salt, and pepper. Whisk well. Place the remaining ingredients in a large bowl, pour the vinegar mixture over, and mix well.

Serves 4 to 6

224	Calories
5.1 g	Protein
17.6 g	Carbohydrates
15.7 g	Fat
63%	Calories from Fat
2.3 g	Fiber
150 mg	Sodium
0 mg	Cholesterol

Creamy Carrot Soup

❧ ❧

4 tablespoons extra-virgin olive oil
6 carrots, thinly sliced
1½ onions, thinly sliced
2 teaspoons honey
1 teaspoon dried thyme
⅛ teaspoon allspice
4 cups chicken broth
⅛ cup orange juice
⅛ cup lemon juice

PREPARATION TIME:
Less than 1 hour

The herbs and spices in this creamy soup give it a very warming flavor. You might sprinkle the soup with fresh chopped cilantro or parsley, if desired.

Heat the oil and sauté the carrots and onions 8 minutes, until just softened. Add honey, thyme, and allspice and sauté another 2 minutes to release flavors. Add broth, bring to a boil, then cover and simmer 20 to 25 minutes, until carrots are very soft. Purée the soup in a blender; return to the pot. Stir in the juices and season with salt and pepper if desired.

Serves 4 to 6

147	Calories
2.7 g	Protein
14.6 g	Carbohydrates
9.3 g	Fat
57%	Calories from Fat
1.6 g	Fiber
107 mg	Sodium
0 mg	Cholesterol

Thyme Chicken

๛ ๙

1½ teaspoons fresh chopped
    thyme leaves
 2 cups plain yogurt
½ cup Dijon mustard
½ teaspoon salt
½ teaspoon pepper
 1 (2½-pound) chicken cut
    into parts

PREPARATION TIME:
Less than 30 minutes
(plus baking time)

This is a wonderful and simple way to prepare chicken. Prepare a simple vegetable while it bakes.

Preheat oven to 450 degrees. Mix the thyme with the yogurt, mustard, salt, and pepper and spread into two dishes. Roll the chicken pieces in the mixture and bake, uncovered, for 40 to 45 minutes.

Serves 4

472	Calories
49.4 g	Protein
11.0 g	Carbohydrates
24.6 g	Fat
47%	Calories from Fat
0.0 g	Fiber
1275 mg	Sodium
134 mg	Cholesterol

Cooking with Herbs

Thyme Rice Stuffed Tomatoes

8 ripe tomatoes
1 cup rice, cooked
1½ tablespoons fresh
    chopped thyme, or
    2 teaspoons dried
2 teaspoons fresh chopped
    basil, or 1 teaspoon
    dried
2 teaspoons fresh chopped
    oregano, or
    1 teaspoon dried
½ teaspoon salt
½ teaspoon freshly ground
    pepper
3 cloves garlic, minced or
    chopped
8 tablespoons extra-virgin
    olive oil

PREPARATION TIME:
Less than 30 minutes
(plus standing and
    baking time)

With a salad, this makes a filling vegetarian meal.

Cut the tops off the tomatoes and reserve. Scoop the seeds and pulp, and transfer to a large bowl. Combine cooked rice with the herbs, salt, pepper, garlic, and half of the olive oil. Mix well and set aside for 40 minutes or longer. Lightly salt the insides of the tomatoes and turn onto paper towels to drain.

Preheat oven to 350 degrees. Scoop the excess salt from the tomatoes and fill with rice mixture. Replace tops of the tomatoes, then drizzle with remaining olive oil. Bake for 1 hour. For better flavor, baste occasionally during baking.

Serves 4 to 6

241	Calories
2.5 g	Protein
18.1 g	Carbohydrates
18.6 g	Fat
69%	Calories from Fat
2.4 g	Fiber
193 mg	Sodium
0 mg	Cholesterol

Index

❦ ❧

Turkey burgers with Mushroom-Dill Wine Sauce, 128
Turnips, Vegetable Broth, 18

U
Ulcers, 12
 calendula for, 7
Urinary tract infections, 11

V
Valerie's Pumpkin Bread, 72
Varicose veins, 7
Vegetables, 6. *See also* specific types
 Broth, Vegetable, 18
 with Dill Sauce, 121
 Gingered Vegetable Stir-Fry, 162
 Mexican Vegetables, 148
 Salad with Cilantro and Lemon, Vegetable, 95
 Stew with Anise and Cilantro, Vegetable, 27
Vegetarian Pie with Cilantro and Anise Seed Cheese Crust, 26
Vinaigrette
 Basic Herb Vinaigrette, 20
 Daikon and Red Pepper Salad with Tarragon Vinaigrette, 241
 Fennel Daikon Salad with Lemon Vinaigrette, 131
 Green Onions and Tomatoes in Raspberry Vinaigrette, 213
 Jicama Bean Salad with Chipotle Vinaigrette, 106
 Summer Salad with Lemon Vinaigrette, 207
Vinegars, 4. *See also* specific types

W
Walnut oil, 4
 Asparagus with Ginger-Lemon Dressing, 159

Cod with Cucumber-Mint Sauce, Grilled, 185
Salmon with Walnut, Dill, and Tarragon, 240
Walnuts
 for cholesterol reduction, 11
 Curried Chicken Salad, 111
 Lemon Basil Ravioli, 38
 Pompano with Mint Pesto, Grilled, 184
 Salad with Peas, Walnuts, and Mint, 181
 Salmon with Walnut, Dill, and Tarragon, 240
 Valerie's Pumpkin Bread, 72
Warm Gingered Rice Salad, 163
Warm Pasta and Basil Salad, 32
Warm Potato Salad with Dill, 117
Watercress, 6
Watermelon
 cancer, help for, 10
 Jicama and Melon Salsa, 63
Wheat bran, 10
White wine vinegar, 4
Wicklund, Valerie, 72
Wild Rice Salad with Rosemary, 217
Wine
 for heart disease, 12
 vinegars, 4

Y
Yams, 10
Yogurt, 5
 Black Bean Dip, 62
 Chervil Cream Dressing, 56
 Chicken with Chile-Yogurt Sauce, 108
 Cold Cucumber Soup, 123
 for colds, 11
 Curried Chicken Salad, 111

Dilled Bean and Sweet Pepper Salad, 118
Halibut in Lemon-Dill Cream Sauce, 122
as immune system booster, 12
Pumpkin Soup, 189
Raita, Cucumber-Mint, 178
Sage and Garlic Potatoes, 228
Salmon with Walnut, Dill, and Tarragon, 240
Thyme Chicken, 260
Vegetables with Dill Sauce, 121
Warm Potato Salad with Dill, 117

Z
Zester, citrus, 1
Zucchini
 Carrots and Zucchini
  with Herb Dressing, 59
  with Herb Sauce, 209
 Chicken and Zucchini with Almond Pesto, 147
 with Corn and Herbs, 170
 Curried Zucchini Soup, 66
 Herb and Cheese-filled Zucchini, 174
 with Herbs and Sour Cream, 256

Index

INTERNATIONAL CONVERSION CHART

These are not exact equivalents: they've been slightly rounded to make measuring easier.

LIQUID MEASUREMENTS

American	Imperial	Metric	Australian
2 tablespoons (1 oz.)	1 fl. oz.	30 ml	1 tablespoon
¼ cup (2 oz.)	2 fl. oz.	60 ml	2 tablespoons
⅓ cup (3 oz.)	3 fl. oz.	80 ml	¼ cup
½ cup (4 oz.)	4 fl. oz.	125 ml	⅓ cup
⅔ cup (5 oz.)	5 fl. oz.	165 ml	½ cup
¾ cup (6 oz.)	6 fl. oz.	185 ml	⅔ cup
1 cup (8 oz.)	8 fl. oz.	250 ml	¾ cup

SPOON MEASUREMENTS

American	Metric
¼ teaspoon	1 ml
½ teaspoon	2 ml
1 teaspoon	5 ml
1 tablepoon	15 ml

OVEN TEMPERATURES

Fahrenheit	Centigrade	Gas
250	120	½
300	150	2
325	160	3
350	180	4
375	190	5
400	200	6
450	230	8

WEIGHTS

US/UK	Metric
1 oz.	30 grams (g)
2 oz.	60 g
4 oz. (¼ lb)	125 g
5 oz. (⅓ lb)	155 g
6 oz.	185 g
7 oz.	220 g
8 oz. (½ lb)	250 g
10 oz.	315 g
12 oz. (¾ lb)	375 g
14 oz.	440 g
16 oz. (1 lb)	500 g
2 lbs.	1 kg